GARDEN YOURSELF HAPPY

GARDEN YOURSELF HAPPY

Jonny Hincks

A quirky, practical guide to keeping you and your garden thriving

EBURY PRESS

CONTENTS

PART 1: MY GARDENING JOURNEY 6

1. How It All Started: From Pocket Money to Plant Obsession 9

2. My Gardening Philosophy: Keep It Simple, Fun and Stress-Free 19

PART 2: GARDENING HACKS, SEASONAL CHECKLISTS AND TO-DO LISTS 32

3. Getting Prepared: Start Simple, Stay Consistent and Make Gardening Work for Real Life 35

4. Spring: Prepping for Growth 49

5. Summer: Keep It Alive (Without Watering 24/7) 67

6. Autumn: Prepping for Next Year 87

7. Winter: Low-Effort Gardening and Planning for Next Year 111

PART 3: STEPPING UP YOUR GARDENING SKILLS 132

8. Essential Lawn Care Tips 135

9. Mulching, Weeding and Keeping Things Tidy 157

10. Pruning and Deadheading 175

PART 5: ASK JONNY 210

12. Your Biggest Gardening Questions – Answered! 213

13. Gardening Myths: Separating the Weeds from the Wisdom 229

14. From Shed Pride to Seeds of Influence 243

Conclusion: Stay Green, Stay Gorgeous 251

PART 4: GARDENING WITH KIDS AND FAMILY FUN 192

11. Growing Together: The Family Garden 195

1

MY GARDENING JOURNEY

1
HOW IT ALL STARTED:
From Pocket Money to Plant Obsession

Some people fall in love with gardening as adults. For me, it started long before I even knew what gardening really was. I didn't grow up with a trowel in one hand and a copy of a gardening magazine in the other, but I did have something better: family holidays to Holland and a grandma who taught me the difference between a dandelion and a daffodil (and wasn't afraid to tell me off when I got it wrong!).

One of my earliest, most vivid memories is standing in a tulip field just outside Uden, a little town nestled in the south of the Netherlands. I must only have been five or six, but I remember it hitting me like a lightning bolt: *My God, these things are real. They're actually growing.* As a child, seeing that kind of colour, row after row of red, orange, pink and yellow tulips stretching out to the horizon, felt like stepping into a painting.

Uden itself isn't some huge bustling city. It is small, friendly and totally in love with flowers. It has that classic Dutch charm: neat little brick houses with well-kept front gardens, cycling paths everywhere, and a sense that everyone, no matter how small their space, knew how to make things grow. It wasn't about being fancy; it was just part of life. Even as a kid, I could feel how much the Dutch valued nature. Their gardens weren't just somewhere to sit, they were places to live.

I remember standing in that field, tulips taller than my little legs, staring out at windmills in the distance and feeling something. Awe, maybe. Wonder. A little hint of what would become a full-blown obsession years later. That was the moment. The seed was planted – literally and metaphorically.

The thing is, gardening in Holland is like a national sport. Much like the Brits, the Dutch love a good front garden. They adore their plants. But there's a calm confidence to it – it's not showy, it's just what you do. The country is full of open gardens, allotments and little plant stalls on the side of the road. And being surrounded by that culture on our family summer trips, well... it definitely rubbed off.

It's no coincidence that I've always associated gardening with good times. For me, those holidays to Uden weren't just breaks from the school routine. They were filled with family, fresh air, cycling through tulip fields, and sitting around outdoor tables with homemade food and flowers in jars. It all felt incredibly wholesome, even before I knew what 'wholesome' meant.

Looking back, I think that tulip field might've been my first moment of mindfulness. I wouldn't have known the word then, but I remember being completely in that moment. No distractions. Just colour, sunlight and a strange little feeling that plants were kind of magical.

That's the thing about gardening: it can get under your skin before you even realise it. One minute you're kicking about in a field, thinking, 'Wow, these colours are mad,' and the next you're twenty years older, obsessing over soil texture and debating whether to deadhead in the morning or after dinner.

As I got older, when I wasn't gallivanting around tulip fields in Holland, I was earning my pocket money in a much less glamorous, but just as important patch of earth: my nan's garden.

My nan was getting older. I called her 'Oma' (Dutch for grandma), and like most nans' gardens in the nineties, hers was a well-loved, slightly over-planted jungle of hanging baskets, clipped lawns and borders that definitely didn't weed themselves. She needed help and I needed cash for sweets and Pokémon cards (I'm still into those, by the way!), so a deal was struck.

Here's the thing though: if you pulled out the wrong plant, you knew about it. Oma had no problem giving me a proper telling-off if I mistook one of her prized perennials for a weed. I learned pretty quickly to tell the difference between a dandelion and a delphinium, not through books or YouTube tutorials, but through trial, error and a very expressive Dutch-British woman with high standards.

She had a tidy little lawn, and I was in charge of keeping it that way. Edges trimmed, grass cut, borders weeded. There was a bird bath in the middle, a proper centrepiece, and baskets everywhere, overflowing with trailing lobelia, petunias and fuchsias. It was a floral explosion and she loved it. It's funny, looking back now. Hanging baskets are a bit of a family signature. Oma adored them. My mum adored them. And, yep, I'm still trying to get mine to look half as good as theirs.

I can still picture it: me with a trowel that was way too big for my hand, sweating over a stubborn root, muttering under my breath while Oma watched from the kitchen window with a cuppa. And yet... I loved it. I loved being outside. I loved the little victories, like clearing a border and standing back to admire the neatness. And I *really* loved that I was getting paid to do something that didn't feel like a chore.

Nan wasn't a veg grower, flowers were her thing, but she passed on loads of little lessons. Water in the morning, not at night. Deadhead as you go. Don't plant too close together, even if you don't think it'll 'fill out'. And, of course: if you're not sure what it is, *don't yank it out*. She'd sometimes get plant names muddled up (English wasn't her first language), so we'd make up nicknames together. I wish I could remember some of them now; they'd be perfect for this book. But what I do remember is the laughter, the learning and the quiet pride I felt every time she said, 'That looks lovely, Yonny.' She could never pronounce her Js.

And then, just as I was starting to really enjoy those little garden jobs, life threw me a curveball.

I was ten when my mum sat me down and told me she had cancer.

There's no guidebook for that moment. No how-to manual for suddenly growing up, for taking on responsibility when all you want to do is ride your bike and argue about what's for tea. Life shifted overnight, and so did I. I had to step up at home, for my younger brother, for my dad, and oddly enough, one of the first places I found comfort in all the chaos... was the lawn.

Gardening had already been gently seeping into my life through my nan, but this was different. Now, it was my job to take care of the garden, especially the grass. I became the unofficial 'Head of Lawn', armed with a basic mower, a determination to impress and a growing love for neat stripes.

Mum, despite everything she was going through, loved her garden. And she was the undisputed queen of the hanging basket. Honestly, they were outrageous, overflowing, Technicolor explosions that practically dripped with blooms. Geraniums, trailing fuchsias, busy lizzies... you name it, she could make it flourish. No garden-centre basket ever came close to Mum's. I still try to recreate them, year after year, and none ever quite match up. But I keep doing it anyway. It's my little tribute to her.

She also loved Wimbledon, and summer was her season. There was nothing she liked more than sitting out in the garden, cold drink in hand, watching the tennis and admiring her baskets. Even now, when summer rolls around and the grass is green and the baskets are blooming, I swear I can still hear her voice, gently correcting me on how to water or trim something.

As I got older, the garden became more than a place of chores, it became my escape. A little patch of calm. I used to push the mower back and forth, watching the lines appear, and feel the weight of everything lift, even if just for a while. It wasn't just about grass. It was about control in a life that felt uncontrollable. It was about peace, when everything else felt like chaos.

She passed away when I was 18. Eight years of fighting, of hope, of heartbreak. My youngest brother was only eight. I suddenly found myself in a house full of men. My dad, my older brother, my little brother, and very little communication. Feelings didn't get discussed. Emotions weren't something we really knew how to handle. But I had two things that helped me cope: the gym and the garden.

The gym gave me strength. The garden gave me stillness.

And honestly, that balance still defines who I am. My day off now usually features gym in the morning, garden in the afternoon. And always, always mowing the lawn with those crisp clean lines. It grounds me. Connects me. Reminds me of where I started and how far I've come.

For a while after Mum passed, I lost the love for gardening. The family garden had been hers, and it felt wrong to touch it. I kept the lawn neat, that was my job, but the rest of it I left. I didn't want to change her space. I didn't want to 'move on' from her. So I didn't plant. I didn't weed. I just cut the grass. And for those couple of years, that was enough.

But eventually, a new garden and a new chapter called.

THE FIRST HOUSE: PLANTING MY ROOTS

I bought my first house at 23 with my then-girlfriend Jen (now my wife – proof that gardens do help you grow things that last!). We didn't exactly pick a dream home. It was more of a fixer-upper, and by that I mean *everything* needed doing. One winter, I found myself standing in what should have been the bathroom, roofless, while snow fell in around me. That's when I realised two things: 1) we were slightly mad, and 2) there's a fine line between character building and frostbite.

Because we couldn't afford a skip, the garden became the unofficial dumping ground for the renovation. Brick rubble, broken bits of tile, abandoned bathroom fittings, you name it, we heaped it in the garden. Every time I added to the pile, a little part of me winced. I couldn't shake the guilt that I was destroying nature. I felt like I was suffocating something that had the potential to be beautiful. Even under all that chaos, I knew the garden was quietly waiting for its moment.

After about six months of beans-on-toast, blood, sweat and borderline tears, we had the house sorted enough to breathe. And then it was time for the garden. Finally.

It was a classic long, thin, terraced garden with a big silver birch off to one side and a patchy stretch of grass trying its best to stay alive. No borders. No shape. Just grass, trees and potential. I knew most of the basics about gardening and I was buzzing. I had a blank canvas.

I did what anyone would do. I turned to Monty Don.

Every Friday night, I parked myself in front of the telly and watched *Gardeners' World*. Back then, it was just half an hour long, but that half hour felt sacred. Monty became my mentor. He didn't know it, obviously, but I was basically enrolled in the Don School of Gardening. His calm, no-fuss style made gardening feel approachable. He never made it feel like you had to be perfect, just present.

I also hit the internet hard. Websites, books, forums, anywhere I could soak up plant names, sun-vs-shade rules, bulb-planting guides, soil tips... you name it. I was a sponge. I planted my first conifer (and I think I nailed it!). Within six weeks, I was absolutely hooked. Obsessed.

Then, just as I was starting to get into the swing of it... we sold the house.

Classic, isn't it? All that effort, all that learning, and not a single border finished. If I could give any advice here, it's this: *always* take pictures of your work before you move house. Because all I've got from that garden is memories and one very confused-looking conifer in someone else's garden now.

HOUSE NUMBER TWO: GROWTH, GRIT AND GARDEN

House number two felt like a fresh start. This time, the place didn't need quite so much doing up (thankfully!). That meant one thing: I could throw myself straight into the garden. And trust me, I was ready.

This garden was a bit of a puzzle, shape-wise. It was a small, south-facing space set across different levels, like a garden that couldn't decide what it wanted to be. A conservatory led onto a patio, then steps up to a lawn, and beyond that a small triangular wedge where the sun hit hardest. South-facing gardens can be a blessing and a curse. You get the best of the sunshine, but so does every weed, pest and crispy-leaved plant. Hydration becomes a full-time job.

Now, if I'm being honest, my favourite aspect for a garden is west-facing. You get a lovely golden-hour glow in the evening without being blasted all day long. But I was determined to make this south-facing garden sing.

First things first: I needed a decent shed. Not just a slap-up shack, something smart. A shed with swagger. I popped it at the bottom of the garden as my hub, a kind of potting palace where I could pretend to be more organised than I actually was. Then came the planting.

I planted my very first apple tree here, a Granny Smith, which I picked because it's self-fertile. I had no idea if any neighbours had apple trees, so better safe than sorry. And the first time I saw apples forming on *my* tree, I felt like a proud parent. It's wild how something so small can give you that deep feeling of achievement. (And let's be real, they tasted better because I grew them.)

This garden, despite being smaller, felt like mine in a way the first one never did. I felt comfortable. It was the first place where I could slow down and try things properly. I experimented with tomatoes, cucumbers, courgettes, anything that looked remotely edible. And – here's where it gets a bit nerdy – I became truly *obsessed* with my lawn. Not just cutting it, *caring* for it. Scarifying, aerating, feeding, edging. I was Googling fertiliser ratios at 10pm like it was revision for a life exam. I started learning how to stripe it properly. I swear to you, getting the perfect line became my personal Everest. I'll go into full lawn care geek-mode later in this book. I bet you can't wait!

I also love a shady, woodland-style border. South-facing gardens don't exactly scream woodland vibes. But I got creative. I had a row of conifers at the bottom of the garden, so I lifted the lower branches to let in some dappled light underneath and turned that area into a mini woodland oasis.

This was also the house where my daughter, Lissy, was born. One of my favourite memories from this garden is her waddling barefoot across the lawn for the first time. I remember telling her (probably too seriously for a toddler), 'No shoes on the grass, please!' Gotta start them young, right?

That moment stuck with me. The garden wasn't just a place for plants anymore, it was where life happened.

First steps, sun-soaked lunches, tiny fingers helping me 'plant' things (and occasionally dig them back up again). It cemented what I already knew deep down: gardening wasn't a hobby for me anymore. It was part of who I was.

By the time baby number two was on the way, my boy Max, our little triangle garden was starting to feel a bit tight. I'd crammed in as much greenery as possible, but when you're trying to juggle a lawn obsession, two kids and dreams of bigger borders, it was clear: we needed more space.

HOME, IN EVERY SENSE OF THE WORD

So, off we went to house number three – our current home, and the garden you probably know from my social media. When we moved in, the garden was… well, let's just say it had 'potential'. It was a basic rectangle: scraggly lawn, gravel paths that looked like a sad Zen garden, and a tin shed that had seen better decades. There were no borders, no structure and absolutely no personality. I walked out onto that lawn and thought, 'Right, this is going to take some serious graft.' And then I immediately got a wave of anxiety over just how bad the lawn was. For a lawn-lover, it was a crime scene. Brown patches, tufts of something pretending to be grass, moss doing the conga in the corner. Honestly, I felt personally offended.

The house needed a lot of work, too, so gardening had to wait a bit. Most of our budget went into building an extension. But you know me, I couldn't leave the garden alone for long. So I did the next best thing: I started buying plants and keeping them in pots. My patio slowly turned into a mini nursery. If there was a sale on perennials, I was there. Compost going half price? I'm bulk buying. I basically had a garden centre operating from my back doorstep, just waiting for its moment.

And just when I thought I was finally ready to begin transforming the space… I went and snapped my Achilles tendon playing rugby.

Now, if you've never snapped an Achilles, let me save you the suspense: it's painful, dramatic and absolutely ruins your gardening plans. I needed surgery and crutches, and suddenly the idea of digging out borders or laying a patio felt like a distant fantasy. It hit me hard. Gardening was my therapy. My escape. I was worried sick about my mental health. Not being able to train at the gym, not being in the garden, and not being able to work as a firefighter (my day job). It felt like my whole outlet for stress had been taken away.

That's when I rang the Fire Fighters Charity. I explained I was worried about my mental health, and I'll never forget what the person on the phone said: 'What's stopping you from still doing something?' And they were right. I was on crutches, not in a coma.

So, I adapted. I started doing seated upper-body sessions at the gym. I hobbled around the garden, slowly, planting what I could, planning what I couldn't. (Let's just say I became very good at dragging compost bags around with one foot.) And, because I'm nothing if not stubborn, I ended up building an entire patio in front of my shed *while still recovering*. Maybe not the smartest move, but we'll call it 'occupational therapy'. (I also have a very handy brother-in-law who helped!)

Once the shed was up and the patio was down, it was 'go time'. The dream woodland border I'd been mentally designing for years was finally going to happen. I had plants that I'd been nurturing in pots for two years: hostas, ferns, astilbes, brunnera, Japanese forest grass, acers. Every one of them had a home waiting for them. That border went in first. Honestly, it felt like I was planting part of myself into that soil. A calm, shaded haven where I could relax, reflect and just breathe. Working with my heavy clay soil wasn't easy (spoiler: it never is), but with well-rotted manure, grit and patience, I turned it into a thriving, loamy base for that whole border to come to life.

At the same time, I tackled the sunnier, south-facing areas and started bringing in prairie-style plants like echinacea, rudbeckia and grasses like miscanthus and pennisetum. This was a garden of contrasts: lush, green shade and hot, bold sun. It felt like it was finally coming together.

And then there was the lawn. Oh yes. My Everest. After levelling it, top-dressing it, scarifying it within an inch of its life, I slowly brought it back to life. Stripe by stripe. Feed by feed. This time, I had years of lawn care research under my belt and a decent pair of shears for creating those sharp, crisp edges. If you follow me online, you know I don't mess about with my lawn. I even joke that mowing is my meditation. But honestly? It's true. There's something about the hum of the mower, the smell of cut grass and the rhythm of back-and-forth stripes that helps me switch off like nothing else.

This garden has grown with us. It's where my wife and I sit with a drink on summer evenings. It's where our second child Max took his first steps. And it's where I've found not just a hobby, but a real source of calm, creativity and joy. Every plant has a story. Every patch of lawn has been fought for. Every border is a chapter in my journey.

And I wouldn't change a thing.

FROM MY GARDEN TO YOURS

If you've stuck with me this far, thank you and welcome to the beginning of something special. For me, gardening isn't just a hobby. It's been a thread that's quietly stitched itself through every phase of my life. From childhood tulip fields in Holland to a lawn obsession sparked by grief, from hanging baskets that remind me of my mum to striped lawns that help me feel human – it's all been part of the journey.

I didn't plan to be 'that gardening guy' when I was a kid. I didn't even plan it as an adult. It just kind of happened... quietly, and then all at once. One minute I was mowing Nan's lawn for pocket money, and the next I was building a garden that helped me recover from injury and find peace again.

That's the beauty of gardening. You grow into it. It doesn't matter how much you know or don't know when you start. You learn as you go. You fail sometimes. (Trust me, I've lost more plants than I care to admit. RIP to the hydrangea that never stood a chance.) But even in the flops, there's something good. A laugh, a lesson, a story.

So if you're reading this thinking, 'I don't really know what I'm doing,' then good. That's where all the best gardeners start. You're not meant to know everything. You're just meant to start.

And that's why I've written this book. Not to overwhelm you with Latin names and rigid schedules, but to help you realise that you can absolutely do this. Whether you've got a big garden, a tiny yard, a few pots on a balcony, or just the itch to get growing, this is for you.

My approach is simple:

- A little, often.
- Learn by doing.
- Enjoy the ride.

Don't worry about making it perfect. Just make a start. And when in doubt, mow the lawn.

Let's grow, together.

2
MY GARDENING PHILOSOPHY:
Keep It Simple, Fun and Stress-Free

If there's one thing I want you to take away from this book, it's this: gardening shouldn't feel like a chore.

We live in a world where we feel that everything needs to be perfect. Perfect lawns, perfect borders, perfect photos for Instagram (more on this later!). But real-life gardens? They're messy, sometimes overgrown, sometimes full of weeds, sometimes full of toys, and sometimes your best plant drops dead overnight for no apparent reason. And that's absolutely normal. It's not just about the end result, it's also about the journey. I know that sounds cheesy, but it's true. Don't let the setbacks get to you – they'll happen, but growth takes time and it's all part of learning.

I learned this the hard way.

When I bought my first house, I was convinced that I'd transform my new plot into a show garden overnight. I'd binge-watch gardening shows, take furious notes, and then spend entire weekends digging, planting, rearranging... until my back gave out and I was completely knackered. By Sunday night, I'd slump onto the sofa, covered in soil and feeling defeated because the garden still looked nothing like the ones I'd seen on TV.

I had no plan, was trying to do too much, too quickly, and I'd turned gardening – the thing I loved – into yet another source of stress. I forgot the whole reason I loved it in the first place. Gardening is one of those things that can be fun and relaxing. A chance to unplug and unwind. At its heart, gardening is supposed to be one of the simplest joys in life. It's getting your hands into warm soil on a spring day, the smell of tomatoes in a greenhouse, the quiet buzz of bees drifting through lavender, or the peace and quiet of an early morning garden walk.

When I let go of the idea that my garden had to be perfect and everything had to be done immediately, it all changed. I started seeing gardening as something to dip into, even if some days I could only spare ten minutes.

It's fine if you only manage ten minutes after work. It's okay if a few weeds slip through. It's normal if your hydrangeas look like they've gone ten rounds with a hairdryer. Gardening should be something that lifts you up, not grinds you down.

So, take a breath. Slow down. Remind yourself that you're not gardening for a magazine shoot, you're gardening for yourself. For your peace of mind, your bit of beauty, your connection to the earth.

And if you're still worried about whether you're 'doing it right', trust me – you are. You're out there, giving it a go. And that's all that matters.

The Power of Small, Consistent Efforts

The beauty of gardening is that even the smallest successes feel like big wins.

**The first flower of the season.
A tomato ripening on the vine.
Catching a whiff of mint as you brush past a pot.**

None of those things need a perfect garden to happen. They just need you to be out there, having a go.

One summer, I was convinced my carrots were a disaster. The tops were spindly and the soil looked bone dry. But when I finally pulled one up, there it was: a perfect little (I mean little) orange veggie. Not actually perfect, but I grew it… and it was delicious. I must have grinned for an hour!

Moments like that remind me why I garden. Not for perfection, but for the small joys that appear when you least expect them.

One of the biggest lessons I've learned in gardening is this: little and often beats big and exhausting. Every time.

When people ask how I keep my garden going around my shifts as a firefighter, raising kids, trying not to forget anniversaries and making time for the gym, the answer is simple: I do small jobs, consistently. That's it. No secret formula. No magic green thumb. Just small steps, taken regularly.

I used to think real gardening meant endless hours in the garden. I'd block out a day, determined to 'sort it all out'. By 10am, I'd be feeling good, tools laid out, a rough plan in my head. By 4pm, my body was sore, I'd have blisters, and I'd feel defeated because the garden still looked a mess and that plan I had in my head was far from reality. Shifting my mindset and being more realistic really helped.

I started approaching gardening in a whole new way that actually allowed balance back into my days. Small, consistent tasks not only made it more enjoyable, but I noticed a huge boost to my mental health. Not only that, the whole family can get involved if you take this approach and it really becomes magical.

MAKING IT WORK WITH REAL LIFE

Let's talk about the common trap: the big weekend blitz. You finally get a free day, the sun's out, and you decide today's the day. You mow the lawn, weed the borders, sow all your seeds, and attempt to prune something massive and angry looking that you've been ignoring all winter. You feel like a legend by teatime. But by Monday? You're stiff, tired and had no time to enjoy your space and rest.

Sometimes, you've got five jobs you could be doing, but you don't know which to tackle first, so you end up doing none of them, or try to tackle parts of all of them. Sound familiar?

The solution? Break it up into manageable chunks. Knowing when to stop is as important as knowing when to start. It means saying, 'Today, I'll just prep that bed,' or 'This evening, I'll water the containers and check for slugs.' That's it. Keep it simple.

Between work, family and trying to have some kind of social life, time is limited. I get it. As a firefighter, a parent and someone who's forever trying to keep life vaguely balanced, I know that free time doesn't just drop into your lap. You've got to grab it in pockets, a few minutes here, a spare half-hour there. Some days you'll manage loads; other times, watering a few pots might be the best you can do. And that's absolutely fine. For me, gardening has become something that supports my wellbeing, so if I know I have a busy week ahead, I'll set some time aside to make sure I can tick off some garden jobs.

This book is built around that philosophy: gardening for real life, not an idealised version where you've got a full day in the sun, your tools are spotless and your plants behave like they do on telly. Real life is school pickups, work meetings, interruptions, house chores and all that stuff! So do what you can, when you can.

I've laid out the seasonal tasks in this book by how much time they take, not just when they need doing. Whether you've got ten minutes before the school run, a lunch break between meetings, or an unexpected quiet hour on a Sunday afternoon, you'll have something you can get stuck into and feel good about afterwards.

Some of my best gardening moments have been in the early morning, pulling weeds in my flip flops and dressing gown, before the kids have even stirred. No schedule, no to-do list, just me and the garden for ten quiet minutes. That's the magic. That's what I want for you too.

The goal isn't perfection it's progress. It's that slow and satisfying transformation that happens when you give a little time, a little love and a little energy to your outdoor space. And it all starts with preparation (more of that in the next chapter, see page 35). The more you understand your garden, your time and yourself, the more this whole thing starts to feel less like work.

LITTLE JOBS ADD UP

One of the brilliant things about gardening is that tiny jobs can make a huge difference if you keep doing them.

> Ten minutes pulling weeds before work.
> A quick deadhead round the borders while the kettle boils.
> Checking the compost bin once a week.
> Spending 20 minutes tying in climbers so they don't smother everything in sight.

Each job on its own doesn't look like much. But stacked up across the week, those small efforts keep the garden ticking over.

In my own garden, there's rarely a day when I do 'nothing'. Even if it's pouring with rain, I'll poke my head into the greenhouse to check for pests or give a seed tray a bit of water. Those little gestures mean that, when the weekend comes, I'm not faced with a jungle of jobs that feels overwhelming.

Your plants may actually prefer this approach too. Here's why:

- **Less stress on plants.** Light, regular pruning helps keep things neat without shocking the plant with a massive haircut all at once.

- **Healthier soil.** Regular mulching and composting keeps soil life thriving instead of exhausting it with huge chemical blitzes.

- **Fewer pests and diseases.** Catch problems early with frequent small checks, rather than discovering a full-blown infestation after ignoring things for weeks.

I've lost count of how many times I've prevented chaos by just spending five minutes checking under leaves. One summer, I spotted blackfly on my broad beans early, squashed them off and saved the whole crop. If I'd left it another week, they'd have taken over.

Here's the most important part: small, consistent gardening builds confidence. You'll start to feel less overwhelmed. You'll notice changes faster. And you'll get those little rushes of satisfaction, those tiny wins that keep you loving gardening rather than dreading it.

I always remind myself: progress, not perfection. Even if the garden's a bit scruffy in places, I know I've been out there, keeping it going, bit by bit. And that's enough.

So, if you're staring out at your garden thinking, 'It's too much,' remember this: **five minutes today is better than zero**. Tomorrow, do five minutes more. Before you know it, you'll look around and think, 'Not bad at all!'

Embracing Imperfection

Let's just say it upfront: dead plants happen!

I don't care how many followers someone's got on Instagram, how perfect their borders look, or how many gold medals they've won at Chelsea. Every gardener has killed plants. It's part of the job.

I've killed more plants than I'd like to admit. My lavender drowned in soggy clay soil. Tomatoes turned into a mouldy mess because I overwatered them. Hydrangeas that went from lush and green to brown and crispy after one summer heatwave and not enough watering. And do not get me started on my buxus bushes!

Once, I decided to plant a whole bed of lupins because they looked spectacular on a TV show. I was so excited. Guess what – not one survived. My heavy clay soil suffocated them. By August, it looked like a patch of dried spaghetti.

Was it embarrassing? Yes. Even more so because I planted them out front for the whole street to see – doh! Did I learn from it? Absolutely. And I'll tell you what, I now walk straight past lupins in the garden centre and tip my hat with respect. We've agreed to go our separate ways.

The idea that there's some perfect, flawless garden out there is a myth. Even the best gardens have their problem areas. There's always a patch that's too dry, a shady corner that refuses to grow anything, or a bed where weeds keep popping back up. In my garden, I've got a border that looks amazing for two weeks in June and then completely falls apart by July. I've stopped fighting it, there's no point letting this cause any stress. Now, I just plant tough perennials there and let them get on with it. Easy fix – problem solved.

MISTAKES ARE HOW WE LEARN

I've learned more from my gardening mistakes than from my successes. Here are some examples:

- Plants that 'thrive in full sun' might still fry in the heat reflecting off my brick patio.
- Watering a lawn every day does more harm than good.
- Planting lavender in clay soil is like trying to grow a cactus in a swamp.

Those failures shaped how I garden now. They make me a better gardener. And crucially, they've made me far more relaxed about it all.

Here's a truth: no one notices your dead plants as much as you do.

Your friends and family aren't wandering around your garden going, 'Ooooh, shame about that dead hydrangea.' They're looking at the bits that are beautiful, smelling the flowers, or even just enjoying being outside with you.

We had a big family BBQ last year, and half my pots looked amazing. The other half were wilted disasters because they hadn't had enough water in the heat of summer. Did anyone care? No. They were too busy enjoying the sausages and the sunshine.

INSTAGRAM VS REALITY

These days, it's easy to feel inadequate as a gardener. Social media is full of perfectly edged lawns, immaculate raised beds and flower borders bursting with blooms in coordinated colours.

And don't get me wrong, I love seeing those gardens. I find them inspiring and uplifting. But I also know that behind every perfect Instagram photo is usually:

- a pile of tools shoved just out of shot,
- a patch of weeds conveniently cropped out,
- a gardener who is probably, at some point, as baffled by plants as the rest of us,
- and, in my case, a family laughing their socks off because it usually takes about 11 takes to get something right!

In my own videos and photos, I try to keep it real. Yes, I'll show you the good bits, but I'm also the first to admit when something's gone pear-shaped. Because that's what gardening is. A mixture of successes and failures, triumphs and disasters. And that's what makes it fun. I'd rather bring a bit of fun and cheer up someone's day than chase some polished, unrealistic ideal. For me, joy, laughter and messy hands beat a flawless flower bed every time.

So let me say this loud and clear: **you're allowed to get things wrong.**

You're allowed to plant something in the wrong spot. You're allowed to prune something too hard. You're allowed to lose a few plants over winter. It's all part of learning about your garden and learning as a gardener.

And here's the best bit: plants are surprisingly forgiving. Many bounce back from neglect. Others might die, but they leave a space for you to try something new.

Whenever I lose a plant, I try to remember one thing: dead plants can become compost. They feed the soil for the next season. They're not wasted. They're part of the cycle. It's nature's way of saying, 'Never mind, try again.'

So, the next time you see a crispy brown stem where a lush plant used to be, take a breath. Learn the lesson. And remember that no gardener – not me, not anyone – gets it right every time.

How the Outdoors Became My Escape

I've always loved the outdoors. Even as a kid, I was happiest mucking about in the garden, 'helping' my grandparents weed beds or earning pocket money cutting grass. But I didn't truly realise what gardening meant for my mind until I got older and until life started throwing a few more challenges my way.

Most people know me as a gardener now, but I'm also a firefighter. It's a job I love, but let's be honest, it comes with its share of stress. Long shifts, adrenaline spikes, tough calls. There are days when my brain feels as though it's been put through a tumble dryer.

For me, gardening became more than a hobby. It became a way to switch my brain off from the noise. I can go from a night shift, full of flashing lights and chaos, straight into my garden the next morning. The second I'm out there, I feel my shoulders drop. The smell of soil, the sound of birds, even the feel of the trowel in my hand, it grounds me in a way nothing else does.

There's a lot of talk these days about mental health, and rightly so. For me, gardening is my therapy.

It's the one place where I feel completely myself. I don't have to be Jonny the firefighter, or Jonny the weird bloke off Instagram. I'm just me, mucking about in the soil, trying to convince my roses to behave.

During tough times (and there have been a few), the garden has kept me sane. After a difficult call at work, I'll find myself outside, hands in the compost, breathing in the scent of damp earth. It's impossible to stay wound up when you're surrounded by things quietly growing.

Another thing I love about gardening is how it connects you to the rhythm of the year.

**In winter, you rest.
In spring, everything wakes up.
In summer, you celebrate.
In autumn, you reflect and prepare.**

No matter what's happening in the world, the seasons keep turning. That steadiness is reassuring. It reminds me that life moves on, plants recover, and so do we.

Gardening isn't just something I do. It's part of who I am. It's given me a way to share joy with others, whether that's my kids growing giant sunflowers, creating a retreat for my wife to sit and have a glass of wine, or people online who tell me my videos made them smile after a rough day. It all comes back to my garden.

Sometimes, people say, 'Oh, you must be an expert gardener.' And I always tell them: I'm not an expert. I'm just someone who's found peace, purpose and endless fascination in my space.

This is why I wrote this book. Gardening is about more than plants. It's about connection, calm and those tiny moments that remind you that life can be good, even on the hardest days.

So, if you ever feel overwhelmed, go outside. Touch the soil. Listen to the birds. Let nature help you breathe again. And remember you're not alone – there's a whole world out there waiting to help you find your balance.

How to Navigate This Book: A Seasonal Approach

Alright, so here's something you should know right away: this book is not meant to be read once, put on a shelf and forgotten about. It's meant to be dog-eared, splattered with compost, stuffed with Post-its, scribbled on and possibly even found outside on a garden chair where you accidentally left it in the rain (don't worry, I've done that too).

I've written this book the way I garden: seasonally, practically and with a dash of humour.

I genuinely believe the best way to tackle gardening, especially if you've got a busy life, is to work with the seasons.

The seasons are nature's way of giving us manageable chunks of time. Instead of looking at your garden and thinking, 'Oh crikey, there's so much to do...', break it down into smaller windows of focus (I'll go into this in more detail later):

SPRING
The big wake-up. Planting, pruning, prepping soil. So much promise.

SUMMER
Keeping it alive (without living outside 24/7 with a hose).

WINTER
Low-effort jobs and plotting your next moves from the warmth of the sofa.

AUTUMN
Tidying up, planning ahead, banking seeds for next year.

In my own garden, I always plan my jobs season by season. It stops me feeling overwhelmed and lets me enjoy each stage for what it is. Even in winter, there's something to do – even if it's just flicking through seed catalogues and daydreaming.

USE THIS BOOK HOWEVER YOU LIKE

Some people love reading gardening books cover-to-cover. Others dip in for quick advice. Both ways are perfectly fine.

Here's how I'd suggest using this book:

Feeling inspired? Flip to the seasonal chapter that's relevant right now and see what you could be tackling this week.

Overwhelmed? Head to the checklists and grids at the end of each seasonal section. They're your cheat sheets when you're standing in the garden thinking, 'I've no idea where to start.'

Only got ten minutes? No problem. Check out the Quick Jobs sections in each seasonal chapter for speedy wins.

Got a specific problem? Use the Q&A section where I answer real questions from my followers.

The idea is that this book should fit into your life – not the other way around.

One of my favourite sayings is: *'You don't have to do it all today.'* And that's why this book is broken down into bite-sized pieces. If all you manage one evening is to deadhead a few flowers or check for slugs, that's still progress. Gardening is a journey, not a race.

WHY I'VE INCLUDED THE FUN STUFF

You might notice this book isn't just full of lists and plant advice. Instead, it's full of:

Personal stories.
So you know you're not the only one whose plants occasionally cark it.

Behind-the-scenes bits.
Because gardening – and social media – aren't always as polished as they look.

Quirky humour.
Because if you can't laugh about slug invasions, what's the point?

I wanted this book to feel like we're chatting in your garden over a brew. No jargon, no guilt-tripping, and no pressure to have the perfect garden.

Your garden, your rules. There's no one right way to garden.

Whether you've got a balcony, a small patch of grass, or half an acre, this book is for you. Pick the parts that help you. Ignore the bits that don't. And remember it's your garden, and you're allowed to make it work for your life.

So go ahead. Flip through, scribble notes, dog-ear pages. And whenever you're feeling stuck, just ask yourself:

'What season am I in, and what small thing could I do today?'

That's how I garden. And I promise, it works.

2

GARDENING HACKS, SEASONAL CHECKLISTS AND TO-DO LISTS

3
GETTING PREPARED
Start simple, stay consistent and make gardening work for real life

Before we even get to the fun stuff, like what to plant and where, when to prune, how to bring your garden to life, and so on, let's talk about the foundations of it all: getting prepared. And no, I don't mean blowing the budget on shiny tools or perfectly labelled seed trays. Real preparation is about giving yourself the space and the right tools both physically and mentally to make gardening an enjoyable part of your life, not just something you do in mad, exhausting and stressful bursts when you have people coming over for that first barbecue of the season!

I've seen it time and again, and I admit I've done it myself – people get the gardening bug, dive in at 100 miles an hour, try to tackle everything in one weekend, and then collapse on the sofa with a sore back, a dead lawn and a strong desire never to pick up a trowel again. Or, on the flip side, feel so overwhelmed thinking about where to start that they just… don't. The result? A neglected garden that becomes a source of stress instead of a place of calm, peace and tranquillity.

Here's the truth: the best kind of gardening is the kind that works *for you*. It's not about sticking to some perfect Pinterest board. It's about setting yourself up in a way that fits into your life – messy, unpredictable, real life. Trust me, if I can do it, you can.

When you're properly prepared, you cut out so much of the frustration that can come with gardening. You know where your tools are and which ones you need. You've got compost ready when you need it. You've thought about your space so you know where the sun hits and what the soil's doing. Suddenly, a job that might have felt overwhelming becomes doable. You're not scrambling. You're stepping in with a plan, and you're enjoying the process.

With preparation comes confidence. It gives you a sense of control with a hobby that, let's face it, doesn't always behave the way you want it to! The weather changes, seeds don't germinate, squirrels dig up your bulbs (like my squirrel – we've named him Stephen!), or the kids decide to play a very competitive game of football on your newly seeded lawn… But if you've taken the time to get things in order, you'll be much more ready to roll with those punches and not let them get you down.

Preparation Is More Than Just Tools

Most people think preparation means ticking off a shopping list of stuff: trowel, fork, gloves, compost. And, yes, those things help (more on that later). But real preparation is also about your mindset, your space and how you want it to work for you, and your expectations.

It means asking yourself:

> What do I actually want from this space?
> How much time can I realistically give it?
> What do I enjoy doing – and what do I dread?
> Where does the sun hit? Where does water collect?
> Where is a nice spot to sit with a morning coffee/evening drink?

We'll go into these questions and more in this chapter and I've also included space for you to make notes on your own outdoor space.

Taking the time to understand your garden, even just standing outside with a cuppa and having a proper look, can save you hours of faffing about later. For example, there's no point planting sun-loving tomatoes in the shady corner under the tree. And there's no joy in planning to dig out a massive veg patch if you don't actually like veg that much. Make the garden work for you.

Gardening should be a joy, not a burden. The more thought you put into the early stages, the more freedom and enjoyment you'll have later. And don't worry when things inevitably go sideways, as they sometimes do. You'll be able to adjust without stress, because you started with that good foundation and plan.

WHY PREPARATION MATTERS

Preparation is key, and will help you make the most of whatever spare time you have to get out in your garden. Maybe you've only got ten minutes after work. Maybe you've got a whole Sunday. Maybe you're juggling kids, a job, pets, and trying to remember where you last put your shed keys. That's fine. You don't need to be perfect to be a gardener. You just need to show up in a way that works for you.

As I covered in the last chapter, the 'little and often' approach keeps the momentum going. It stops weeds becoming jungles, keeps your compost aerated and stops jobs piling up into one overwhelming to-do list that you just can't face.

Preparation is what makes that possible. It's what turns a vague idea of 'doing the garden' into a real plan of action, even if it's just popping out in your pyjamas to deadhead the daffodils. Personally, I love an early morning garden walk to start the day off in a positive way.

Take the time to get yourself ready. As I've said, know your space, know your tools and know your limits. That's where good gardening begins and that's when it starts to become something you look forward to doing. Consider things such as:

- How much time can I realistically spend gardening each week?
- What points of the day or week am I most likely to have time to spend on the garden?
- What parts of gardening bring me joy?
- Am I setting realistic goals for my time?
- Do I prefer short regular sessions, or longer more infrequent ones?
- What could I simplify or change to enjoy gardening more?

These reflections will help you avoid becoming overwhelmed. You'll then be able to step into the garden with confidence and a realistic plan that supports your lifestyle and goals.

Get to Know Your Space Before You Start

Before you lift a single tool or buy your first seed packet, you need to **understand the space you're working with**. This isn't about being technical or scientific, it's just about observation.

Every garden, balcony, patio or window box has its own microclimate and quirks. Some areas catch all the morning light but are shaded by next door's garage by 2pm (how rude). Others are suntraps in summer and iceboxes in winter. Some spots stay bone dry no matter how much it rains, while others stay soggy underfoot long after the rain has passed.

The key to gardening isn't about doing more, it's about working *with* your space, not against it. So, let's walk through the simple steps to truly get to know your garden and make the most of it.

I've left some space on the page at each stage for you to make notes about your own garden – I want you to make this book your own... get soil on the pages, spill tea on it while you look at your lovely lawn... this is your personalised handbook for your garden that you can keep referring back to. If you're short on time or are a more confident gardener already, there's a speedier audit on page 46 that you can fill in.

 ## Where Does the Sun Hit and for How Long?

Light is everything in gardening. Most fruiting plants, such as tomatoes, courgettes, strawberries and beans, need **at least 6 hours of direct sun per day** to thrive. That doesn't mean blazing sunshine from dawn to dusk, but a decent stretch of uninterrupted light.

Here's how to check:
- On a sunny day, make a note of where the sun hits in the morning, midday and late afternoon.
- Set timers or reminders and take photos or notes.
- Watch how light moves across beds, walls and pots throughout the day.

It's a bit of effort upfront, but it gives you a realistic idea of which areas are full sun, part shade, or full shade, and that knowledge makes choosing plants ten times easier.

What to plant where:

Full sun (6+ hours): fruit, tomatoes, beans, herbs, wildflowers, lavender, roses, salvia.

Part shade (3–5 hours): leafy greens, spinach, ferns, hostas, geraniums, hellebores, hydrangea.

Full shade (<3 hours): woodland-type plants, such as foxgloves, ferns, pulmonaria and some heucheras. (I must admit, these plants are my favourites!)

If you've got a shady garden, don't stress. There's loads you can grow; you just need to be realistic and choose the right plants for the right places.

Notes
Sunlight in my garden...

....
....
....
....
....
....
....
....
....

Where Does Water Collect and Where Does It Drain?

Water is another key player. It's likely that your garden isn't evenly balanced. Some areas will be spongy after rain, while others dry out quickly. Knowing this in advance helps you avoid planting water-hating plants in boggy corners (and vice versa).

Here's how to check:
Walk around after a rainy day.
- Are there low spots where puddles form?
- Does water run off patios and collect in certain beds?
- Are some areas dry even after a downpour?

Understanding this helps you decide:
- Where to plant moisture-loving plants, such as astilbes, irises and ferns.
- Where to avoid planting delicate herbs or drought-sensitive species.
- Where mulching or soil improvement might help water retention.
- Whether you need to raise beds or add drainage gravel to soggy spots.

We'll go into this more later. For now, just make a note of the type of soil you have and remember that some 'problem' areas, like shady, damp patches, can actually become amazing wildlife habitats if planted intentionally.

Notes
Water in my garden...

....
....
....
....
....
....
....

What's the Soil Like?

Soil is more than just 'dirt'; it's your plants' home, pantry and anchor all in one. The better you understand it, the better your garden will grow.

Here's a quick, no-fuss soil test:
Dig a small hole and grab a handful. Rub it between your fingers.
- If it feels **gritty and loose**, it's probably sandy soil.
- If it feels **smooth and sticky**, it's likely clay-based.
- If it feels **crumbly, rich and earthy**, that's loamy goodness – ideal.

You can also do the **jar test** if you're feeling extra nerdy. Fill a jar with a bit of your soil, some water and a dash of washing-up liquid. Shake it and let it settle. The layers that form (sand, silt, clay) tell you what you're working with. This is also a fun experiment to do with kids!

Soil types and what they mean:
- **Sandy:** drains fast, warms quickly in spring, but loses nutrients. Great for carrots, herbs and Mediterranean plants like lavender. Needs compost to bulk it up.
- **Clay:** holds nutrients well but can be heavy and waterlogged. Roses, beans, hostas and brassicas love it, but improve drainage with compost or grit.
- **Loam:** the holy grail – balanced, fertile and drains well. Lucky you!

No matter what type you've got, adding organic matter, such as homemade compost, leaf mould or well-rotted manure, will improve it. I'll go into this in more detail later.

Want to go one step further?
Try testing your soil's pH. That's its acidity or alkalinity. Most garden plants prefer slightly acidic to neutral soil (around pH 6.0–7.0). However, some – like blueberries, rhododendrons and camellias – thrive in more acidic conditions. You can buy a cheap pH testing kit online or at the garden centre. Just follow the instructions and you'll know exactly what you're working with. It's not essential, but it's handy to know if you've had repeated issues with certain plants not doing well in the same spot.

Notes
Soil in my garden...

....
....
....
....
....
....
....

What Do You Actually Want from Your Garden?

By now, you should have a strong sense of what is in your garden and how it behaves. Now we get to the sometimes-trickier bit (and the bit that gets overlooked far too often). Before you do anything, you need to ask yourself: *What do I want this space to give me?*

These are some questions I asked myself when I first started on my garden. They are also the same ones I come back to whenever I'm making a change.

- **Do you want to grow food?** If so, you'll want sunny spots, compost bins and raised beds or large containers. I grow my tomatoes, peppers and cucumbers in a small greenhouse and it's taken trial and error to get the amounts right, but now we have a good supply of these throughout the summer to add to salads.

- **Looking for colour and beauty?** Think about flower beds, scent and year-round interest. Two of my favourite colours in the garden are purples and whites. I also think the colours complement each other well. Hydrangeas and salvias are my go-to plants and I have many dotted around the garden. For bright pops of colour, I add hanging baskets filled with begonias, fuchsias and petunias. Don't make the mistake I initially did and underwater them. Hanging baskets dry out pretty quickly, so even if there has been rain, give them a daily water.

- **Do you want low maintenance?** Choose perennials, mulch well and steer clear of anything that says 'highly vigorous'!

- **Need kid-friendly zones?** Sandpits, raised veg beds for little hands, hanging baskets that are out of the way, and space to dig and play are your priorities.

- **Craving peace and quiet?** Seating, soft planting and privacy (hedging, trellis, tall grasses) are key. Consider aromatic plants around any seating area. Mine are lined with jasmine and lavender, and this creates a lovely calming atmosphere.

- **What do you want for daytime vs evening?** If you want separate areas, you'll need a lovely sunny spot to soak up the morning rays with a coffee, and later on a comfortable entertaining area where friends and family can join you as the sun sets.

- **Want a wildlife-friendly garden?** Think pollinators, native planting, bird feeders and a water source – even if it's just a washing-up-bowl pond.

Being clear on your goals and limitations will shape everything else: what tools you buy, what jobs you prioritise, and what kind of gardener you become.

Notes
What I want from my garden...

....
....
....
....
....
....
....
....

Essential Tools (and What You Can Skip)

Let's clear something up: **you don't need a shed full of shiny gadgets** to be a good gardener. In fact, too many tools can often make things more confusing. What you need is a small collection of well-made, useful tools that can do most jobs.

THE CORE KIT (WHAT I ALWAYS USE)

- ☐ **Hand trowel** – Your most versatile tool. Perfect for planting, potting, weeding and moving plants from one place to another. Get one with a solid metal blade and a comfy handle, ideally wooden or rubberised. It's also pretty fun to see how many times you can spin it before catching it by the handle! (I always do it first time...)

- ☐ **Hand fork** – Great for loosening soil, mixing in compost and teasing out weeds with delicate roots. Also handy for breaking up clumps in raised beds or pots.

- ☐ **Secateurs** – A sharp pair of secateurs are worth every penny. Use them for pruning, deadheading, trimming herbs and cutting soft stems. Keep them clean and oiled, and they'll last for years.

- ☐ **Watering can** – A standard 10-litre can is enough for most small gardens. A removable rose (the bit that makes the water come out like a shower) is great for watering seedlings and delicate plants.

- ☐ **Gloves** – You'll be surprised how often you use these. Go for breathable ones that give you some dexterity, and maybe a tougher pair for thorny jobs like roses and brambles.

- ☐ **Hoe** – Ideal for tackling weeds quickly and easily – just skim across the soil and cut them off at the root. I always recommend this for no-dig gardeners, too.

- ☐ **Rake** – Not just for leaves – use it to level soil, gather debris and spread compost or mulch evenly over beds.

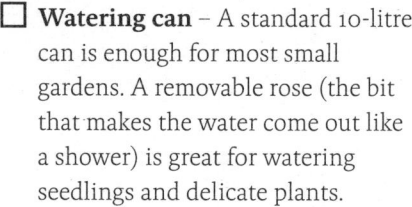
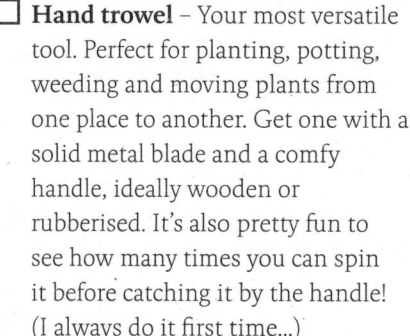

- ☐ **Garden trug or bucket** – Simple but essential. Great for collecting weeds, carrying tools or ferrying compost around the garden.

- ☐ **Long-handled spade and fork** – Great for digging large beds or turning compost.

- ☐ **Sturdy footwear** – Go for waterproof boots or wellies with good grip. Trust me, once you've stood in a slug-filled border in your trainers (or, worse, flip flops), you'll never make that mistake again.

THE NICE-TO-HAVES (HANDY BUT OPTIONAL)

- ☐ **Loppers** (great word – fun to say) – For thicker branches on mature shrubs and trees.

- ☐ **Garden kneeler** – Useful if you're prone to sore knees or like a bit of comfort, but you could always use an old cushion/towel, etc.

- ☐ **Wheelbarrow** – Super-useful if you've got a bigger space or heavy lifting to do.

THE STUFF YOU CAN SKIP (AT LEAST FOR NOW)

- ☐ **Soil thermometers** – Just stick your finger in (hehe). If it's freezing cold, it's not time to plant.

- ☐ **Specialist tools for every job** – You don't need a different trowel for every plant. Simplicity is key.

- ☐ **Battery-powered weeders or pest zappers** – Gimmicks. Not worth it.

Do Your Own Simple Garden Audit

I've always found it super-helpful to do a simple garden audit that brings together the main things I've learned from my preparation, so I can use it to make future plans. On the opposite page, sketch a rough map. It doesn't need to be pretty, just a basic layout of your garden, and then add notes. Take an hour, grab a cuppa and use this page as a notebook. Walk around your garden with these prompts:

- Where are the sunniest and shadiest spots? You can lightly shade over the spots that are often in shade.
- Where does water sit or drain?
- What kind of soil do you have in different areas?
- What plants are already in your garden? Do they seem happy? Do you like these plants?
- What spaces are usable now or are you happy with the layout as is?
- What needs work? Do you have any ideas of what you'd like these areas to be? E.g. place for seating, beds or a compost bin.

You Don't Need to Know it All

One important thing to remember: **don't get stuck waiting until you know everything**. Gardening is not about having the perfect plan. It's about observing, trying, failing, adjusting, learning as you go and feeling better for it.

All you need to do is start. Put on your boots, grab your trowel and give it a go.

GETTING PREPARED

My garden map

Notes

....
....
....
....
....
....
....
....
....
....

4
SPRING
Prepping for Growth

Spring is the season when everything changes. After the darker months, when everything feels a bit stuck and heavy, spring arrives like a deep breath. The days grow longer, the sun begins to feel warm again, and there's a gardening buzz in the air. From the bees rousing to the first daffodils poking their heads up, spring always puts a smile on my face. For gardeners, it's a magical time – and let's be honest, one of the busiest! But don't let that put you off. This chapter is all about getting stuck in without getting overwhelmed, whether you're brand new to gardening or just need a refresher.

I love the spring – the return of the green growth and bulbs starting to bloom mirrors a quiet renewal in my own mind, a lovely reminder that the light is returning and I can spend more time in my own little sanctuary. Gardening, at its heart, is about connection. Connection to your space, to the seasons, and most importantly to yourself. Spring is your opportunity to re-establish that connection and create something beautiful, productive and uniquely yours.

Some of my favourite plants hit their stride in spring. Alliums, bluebells and early clematis bring colour and shape that never get old. And tulips? They're not just flowers to me. They take me straight back to childhood trips to Holland with my family, running through rows and rows of them, with mud on my shoes and a snack in my pocket. Those memories are rooted in my love for this season.

Then there's the lawn. I know, it's a niche obsession, but I'm a self-confessed lawn geek. Spring is when I get to do the first mow, tidy up the edges and dive into my favourite part of lawn care: spring maintenance. There's nothing more satisfying than seeing that rich, green carpet start to wake up again after winter. Yes, I am the kind of person who gets excited about aeration and scarifying. No shame here!

But beyond the blooms and the lawn stripes, there's something deeper at play. As a firefighter, my job is full-on. Physically demanding, mentally tough and emotionally heavy at times. Gardening in spring gives me a way to reset. It's not just a hobby; it's therapy with muddy hands. The garden doesn't talk back, doesn't rush you, doesn't demand perfection. It just responds to my care. After a long shift, stepping outside grounds me. The fresh air, the feel of soil, the rhythm of planting and pruning... it all helps me decompress and process the noise of a busy life.

Spring is when I finally feel like I can move again. It's when the garden becomes my haven. And I want to share that with you – not just the tips and techniques, but the genuine joy and calm that comes from making something grow.

Whether you've got ten minutes or thirty, this chapter will show you how to make the most of those small pockets of time in an organic, easy and chemical-free way. Think of it as gardening that fits into and around *real life*.

So, kettle on, gloves out and let's get growing!

Why Spring Matters

Spring sets the tone for the entire gardening year. Think of it like warming up before a workout: it's the essential prep that makes sure everything that follows runs smoother. (Not that I *always* warm up, let's be honest. But I'm over 40 now, so I should probably start!) In the garden, skipping the spring warm-up isn't worth the risk. This is the moment where everything resets, recharges and kicks into gear.

After the long drag of winter – dark days, soggy ground and garden tools buried under cobwebs – spring feels like someone's opened a window and let the fresh air in. The soil softens, the sun sticks around a bit longer each day, and suddenly things start happening. You'll see buds swelling, shoots pushing through and birds getting cheeky again. Even the weeds are excited (and yes, we'll deal with those too).

Spring isn't just about the plants. It's about momentum. Getting out there now, even for just a few minutes, builds the rhythm that carries you through summer and beyond. The beauty is, you don't need to do everything at once. You don't need to overhaul the entire garden in a single weekend. In fact, I'd recommend that you don't. Spring is about doing a little but often. One bed here, a bit of lawn care there, maybe a sneaky sowing session between rain showers.

If you've had a rough winter physically, mentally or just in general, this is your chance to reconnect. I always say **gardening isn't just about the plants, it's about the person doing the planting**. Spring gives you a fresh start. Not in a 'New Year's resolution' sort of way, but in a grounded, earthy, *get-your-hands-dirty-and-feel-better* kind of way. Whether you've got a balcony with a few pots or a sprawling garden with beds galore, spring says: *'Let's begin again.'*

So, if you've taken it easy over winter (and who doesn't?), this is your chance to get back into a rhythm. And I'll guide you through it, step by step, minute by minute.

We'll start by taking a look at which plants are perfect to plant in this season, in case you're looking to start a new section of your garden or give it a refresh. Next, we'll take a look at what you might already have in the garden that's ready for a prune at this time of year. After that, we'll look at how you can prepare some permanent fixtures of your garden for the year ahead (including my pride and joy: the lawn).

At the end of the chapter, we'll also take a look at natural pest-control options and which gardening jobs are perfect to do in the spring days – from ten-minute tidy-ups to half-hour fixes, we're going to make it work around you.

With natural methods, achievable wins and plenty of room for laughter along the way, let's make this spring the one where you and your garden really thrive.

What to Plant

Spring is when your garden wants to wake up and it's the perfect time to start planting. From vibrant flowers to crunchy veg and aromatic herbs, what you sow now can feed your soul (and your stomach) for months to come. I'll be giving you handy tips on how to keep your favourite spring flowers thriving. And, if you're new to gardening, it's the perfect time to pick a few plants from the list below to start growing.

We talked about having a plan in Chapter 3. Have a look back at your sketch or think about how the sun hits your garden and consider where these plants will do well in your garden.

BULBS, TUBERS AND FLOWERS

These underground powerhouses are the secret to late spring and summer colour.

Gladioli are dramatic flowers with trumpet-shaped blossoms. Known for their height, they can be planted in succession every couple of weeks for a staggered burst of colour. Again, they love full sun and well-drained soil, but keep them well watered. Gladioli are ideal for beginners as they are easy to care for. You'll just need to stake them as they start getting tall.

Lilies are a classic, elegant and fragrant flower with star-shaped blooms. They do like full sun but can tolerate a bit more shade, and prefer a slightly acidic soil that's well drained. They are fairly easy to grow but take a bit longer to make an appearance than gladioli. They'll come back year on year with some TLC. Water at the base, but not too frequently. Just remember: lilies are poisonous to cats (I have two cats, so I don't plant them), but they are beautiful additions for pet-free homes.

Dahlias are one of my favourites. They come in a huge variety of shapes and colours – some small and delicate and others with blooms the size of plates! The leaves can also range from luscious green to a dramatic dark purple. To plant, wait until the risk of frost has passed or start them off in pots indoors. Once ready to plant, pop them 10–15cm deep somewhere that gets 6–8 hours of direct sunlight in well-drained soil, and make sure you don't overwater them before they start to sprout. Don't be worried if not all of them take – I tend to pot up about ten per year, and some just don't work, but the ones that do are worth it.

COOL-SEASON VEGETABLES

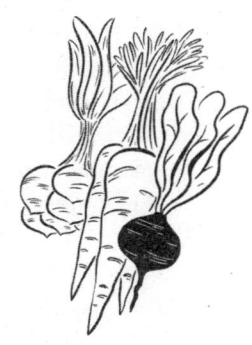

Spring is prime time for cool-season crops. This means it's a great time for planting **lettuce, spinach, broad beans, beetroot, peas, radishes** and **carrots**, all of which thrive in cooler temperatures. They don't love the heat in summer, so get them going now. Sow directly into the ground or in raised beds as soon as the soil is workable. (And don't forget to sow lettuce and radish seeds every couple of weeks, so you have a constant supply of lovely fresh salad!) If you sow them in the spring your radishes can be ready in as little as four to six weeks, lettuce and spinach in around six to eight, and peas, broad beans and carrots in twelve to sixteen weeks.

HERBS

You can't go wrong with a pot of **chives, parsley, thyme** and **mint** on your windowsill or patio. Mint is a thug in the ground, so always plant it in a pot (unless you want it everywhere!). Herbs thrive in free-draining soil and sunshine. Spring sowings are ideal – once they get going, you'll have a fresh supply for months. They're also great for wildlife, especially bees and hoverflies.

PERENNIALS

Perennials are plants that live for more than two years, and come back year on year with the right care. Most bloom for a few weeks each year, which is shorter than annuals, but they make up for it by showing up again and again.

If you're thinking long-term, now is the time to establish reliable perennials, such as **echinacea, rudbeckia** and **hardy geraniums**. The soil is moist, the air is warming and roots will have plenty of time to establish before the summer heat. Dig a generous hole for these, add in some compost, and water them in well. Once settled, these perennials will return each year, stronger and more spectacular.

HARDY ANNUALS

Hardy annuals are plants that complete their life cycle in one year (like all annuals), but these ones are tough enough to tolerate cooler weather.

Spring is the perfect time to sow **calendula**, **cornflowers**, **nigella**, **nasturtiums** and other hardy annuals that tolerate cool nights. These are brilliant for filling gaps in borders, attracting pollinators like bees and butterflies, and giving your plot an instant cottage-garden feel. Most of them can be sown directly where you want them to flower (they're not fussy!), but you can also start them in trays if your soil is too cold. They are low maintenance and resilient. Nigella, in particular, looks amazing sprinkled among perennials – it self-seeds beautifully, too. I have a number of hardy annuals planted to make sure the borders always look full.

What to Prune and How

Pruning isn't just about tidiness, it's about encouraging healthy, productive growth and better flowers. Spring is a great time to prune certain plants while they're still dormant or just starting to break into leaf. If you have any of these types of plants in your garden, make sure to prune them in spring.

ROSES

Spring is prime time for rose pruning, and while it might seem a bit intimidating, roses are tougher than they look. Pruning in spring encourages healthy growth and plenty of blooms later on, so don't be shy with the secateurs.

Here are some general rules:
- Start between late February and early April, once the frosts ease and new buds start to appear.
- Begin by removing any dead stems. Look for anything that is brown or dry rather than green. If you're not sure, scratch the stem with your nail – if it's brown underneath, it's dead and can be removed.
- If you spot any stems that are broken or blackened by insects, snip them back to where the healthy growth is.
- Look out for crossing stems. This is where two stems rub together. Pick the weaker one and cut that one out. Leaving stems crossing can cause the plant's

bark to open and this can lead to disease. Aim for an open shape to help air flow through the plant.
- Always cut just above an outward-facing bud. This is where any new bud is facing away from the middle of the plant. Make sure you cut at a slant to let water drain away, and use clean, sharp secateurs – this will keep your plant healthier.

Depending on the type of rose you have, it may need a more specific approach. Here's a quick guide for different types:
- **Shrub Roses** – Prune by about a third, keeping a balanced, natural shape.
- **Hybrid Teas** – Go a bit harder, cutting back by half to two-thirds, for strong, upright growth.
- **Floribundas** – Trim back by about a third, keeping multiple stems for clusters of flowers.
- **Climbing Roses** – Shorten side shoots to 2–3 buds and tie in main canes horizontally to spread flowering along the stems.
- **Rambling Roses** – Don't prune hard in spring. Just remove dead or damaged wood; save shaping for after flowering in summer.

After pruning, feed with well-rotted compost or manure, and mulch around the base to lock in moisture and build soil health. Keep it organic and your roses will thank you with gorgeous blooms all summer long.

HYDRANGEAS

Hydrangeas are another common character in the garden and they can seem a bit tricky to prune, mainly because not all types are treated the same. But, once you know what you're working with, it's quite straightforward. The key is knowing whether your hydrangea flowers on old wood or new wood, because that changes when and how you prune.

Hydrangea macrophylla (bigleaf, mophead, lacecap varieties)
These are the classic, showy varieties that most people think of when they hear the word 'hydrangea'. They flower on **old wood**, meaning this year's blooms are formed on last year's stems. So if you cut them back too hard in spring, you'll be cutting off the flower buds.

In spring, stick to a light tidy-up:
- **Remove any dead, damaged or spindly growth.** Spindly growth is when the plant is growing, but the stem is weak and thin – this will lead to fewer blooms and floppy stems... no, thank you!
- **Snip off old flower heads** just above a healthy pair of buds.
- **Avoid cutting too far down the stem**, or you risk losing your blooms for the year. You want to cut above the first bud, as that will be this year's flower.

If your plant is very overgrown or woody, rejuvenate it gradually. Cut back one or two of the oldest stems to the base each year to encourage fresh growth without sacrificing all the flowers.

Hydrangea paniculata (such as 'Limelight') and *Hydrangea arborescens* (such as 'Annabelle')

These flower on **new wood**, so they're much more forgiving. You can prune them hard in early spring, before they start actively growing, and they'll still produce beautiful blooms later in the season. These are my favourite and I have multiple plants dotted around the garden!
- Cut stems back to a strong pair of buds about a third from the ground. Look for a large bud and you know it's a good one! This encourages large, lush flower heads and helps maintain a neat shape. Don't worry if it feels drastic – they'll bounce back quickly.
- If you prefer smaller, more manageable flower heads (especially with 'Annabelle', which can flop), prune a bit more lightly, leaving more height.

Hydrangeas thrive with a bit of attention in spring. Once you've nailed the right approach for your type, it's easy. Keep it organic by feeding with compost or a comfrey/nettle tea, and mulch around the base to retain moisture and protect the roots. A little care now means a stunning show later in the year. I have several varieties in my garden, and I love them all!

FRUIT TREES (APPLES AND PEARS)

Spring is a bit of a grace period for apple and pear trees. Ideally, you'd have tackled the main structural pruning in winter while the tree was dormant (see page 119), but if you missed it, don't panic. Early spring still gives you a window for a light tidy-up that can make a real difference without stressing the tree.

Start by stepping back and assessing the overall shape. You're aiming for what's often called a 'goblet shape', an open centre that allows sunlight and airflow to reach all parts of the tree. Good airflow helps reduce the risk of common issues like apple scab and canker, while letting the sun in encourages fruit to ripen evenly later in the season. Here's what to do:

- **Remove any dead, damaged or diseased branches** – these are easy wins and help redirect the tree's energy into healthy growth.
- **Cut out any crossing or rubbing branches**, especially those growing into the centre of the tree.
- **Don't go overboard** – avoid any major structural changes now, as the tree is waking up and needs its energy to fuel new growth and blossom. A heavy prune at this stage can knock it off balance.

Again, it's important to use sharp, clean secateurs or loppers, and make cuts just above a healthy outward-facing bud or branch junction (where two branches meet). Keep tools sterilised between cuts if you're dealing with diseased material. You can use lemon juice and baking soda or one part white vinegar to one part water to clean your tools.

Once you're done, give your trees a good boost by spreading a thick layer of well-rotted compost or mulch around the base (keep it clear of the trunk itself to prevent rot). This feeds the soil, supports beneficial microbes and helps lock in moisture through the growing season.

If you've got younger trees, spring is a great time to check tree ties and supports. Loosen anything that has become tight and replace old stakes, if needed. Let the tree stand strong but supported. If you haven't supported your tree yet, use a strong wooden or metal stake, place it to one side of the tree and push it firmly into the soil so it's steady. Use a soft tree tie and tie it loosely in a figure of eight (one loop around the stake, one loop around the trunk).

Done right, a little spring pruning and care now will reward you with stronger growth, fewer problems and – fingers crossed – a bumper crop later on.

What to Prepare

Preparation is everything. Get your garden ready now and it'll reward you all year long. Here's where to start:

LAWN

Your lawn is waking up, too. Start with a light rake to remove thatch (dead grass) and moss. Next, give it its first cut, but keep the blades high. Follow up with a natural lawn feed, such as seaweed extract, worm castings or a top-dressing of sieved compost. Edging the lawn gives everything a crisp look (and if you're as lawn obsessed as me, it's one of the most satisfying jobs in the garden). I have been known to lay face down in my lawn – I love it!

SOIL

This is the time to give back to your soil. It's the backbone of your garden. Add homemade compost, leaf mould or well-rotted manure to boost fertility and improve structure. Leave any worms you find well alone! Worms will help pull organic matter into the ground and make your plants stronger with healthier growth. Don't dig too much – let nature do the work. No-dig gardening, where you layer compost on top of the soil, is brilliant for encouraging soil life.

COMPOST HEAP

A good compost heap is a gardener's best friend. If you have one, give yours a bit of attention by turning it, balancing brown (dry) and green (wet) materials, and keeping it moist but not soggy. Add things like shredded newspaper, veg peelings, lawn clippings (mixed with dry stuff) and cardboard. Keep out cooked food and meat. If it smells, it needs more brown material. If it's dry, give it a sprinkle of water. Coffee grounds are great to add as a compost ingredient (my wife loves a coffee, so there is no shortage in my house!) – they are a good source of nitrogen, phosphorus and potassium, which are all essential for plant growth.

How to start your own compost heap

- Choose a level, well-drained area of the garden with direct contact to the ground, so worms and bugs can help the process. Some sun can help, but a shaded spot is fine.
- Pop down a layer of twigs and straw to keep air flowing and help drainage.
- Next, add a green layer (wet and fresh) of veg peelings, grass clippings and coffee grounds followed by a brown layer (dry and tough) of leaves, cardboard, shredded paper and small sticks. Aim for half and half. The number of layers will determine the size of your compost heap.
- Keep it moist and turn every few weeks to help things break down faster. Just remember – not too wet and not too dry, and you can't go too wrong!

Natural Pest Control for Spring

Spring also brings back the bugs, and while many are helpful, some need managing. But don't reach for the chemicals! Nature has its own answers. If you're not familiar with what these pests look like, a quick Google will ensure you know what to look out for!

- **Slugs and Snails:** Encourage natural predators like frogs, hedgehogs and birds. Use beer traps or place broken eggshells and copper tape around vulnerable plants. One of my favourite plants is a hosta – unfortunately, slugs love them, so I also use nematodes (see below) to keep the pesky slugs at bay.
- **Aphids:** Blast them off with a strong jet of water. I also use soap and water in a spray bottle – 1 litre of water to 1 teaspoon of mild washing-up liquid. Ladybirds and hoverfly larvae are brilliant allies, so plant things like dill, fennel or yarrow (all spring-friendly plants) to attract them.
- **Vine Weevils:** Keep an eye on container plants. If you suspect grubs, tip out the plant and check the root ball. Use nematodes or keep soil slightly drier. Nematodes are invisible to the eye. They're tiny creatures that eat things like slugs and vine weevils and are a great natural pest control.
- **Cabbage White Butterflies:** Use fine-mesh netting over brassicas and inspect for eggs under leaves. Pick them off by hand (and don't chuck them over next door's fence – ha!).

Quick Jobs for Spring

Spring can feel a bit overwhelming, and can feel like everything comes to life at once, weeds included! Then, suddenly there are hundreds of things to do, but here's the thing, you don't need to give up hours and hours to keep on top of it.

 10-MINUTE JOBS

Only got a few minutes? No problem. These ten-minute jobs will help keep your garden ticking over in spring without the need for a full afternoon in your wellies (or flip-flops in my case). They're the perfect jobs for days when you want to be outdoors but don't have much time.

- ☐ **Deadhead early bloomers like daffodils** – Snip off the faded flower heads to stop the plant putting energy into seed production. But leave the leaves! They're still gathering energy for next year's flowers. Let them die back naturally for the best show next spring.

- ☐ **Sow a row or two of salad leaves in a container** – Grab a trough or even a washing-up bowl, fill it with peat-free compost and sprinkle in mixed leaf seeds. Keep it damp and you'll have fresh salad in a matter of weeks.

- ☐ **Water newly planted shrubs** (use rainwater where possible) – Early spring planting can leave roots thirsty, if there's not enough rain. Fill your watering can from a water butt (or use saved kitchen rinse water, if you're really going green).

- ☐ **Check for pests under leaves and hand-pick if needed** – Flip over the leaves of your leafy plants and have a nose for early signs of aphids, caterpillars or slug eggs. Remove them by hand or gently blast them off with a spray of water.

- ☐ **Turn a corner of the compost heap** – Don't let your compost get lazy. Give one section a quick turn with a fork or aerator. This introduces air and helps the microbes break everything down faster.

SPRING

- [ ] **Brush down tools and hang them up clean** – A quick clean now can save you loads of bother later. Wipe off dirt, sharpen any dull edges, then pop them back where they belong. A tidy shed = a happy gardener.

- [ ] **Pull a few weeds before they seed** – Even just ten minutes of targeted weeding each day keeps the job manageable. Focus on the sneaky ones just about to flower; removing them now means fewer next week.

- [ ] **Sweep your patio or deck** – A simple sweep clears slippery moss, debris and dead leaves. It instantly freshens up the space, and you might even uncover a few forgotten pots while you're at it.

- [ ] **Inspect your greenhouse or cold frame** – Look for signs of mould, pests or condensation build-up. Ventilate when needed and give it a quick tidy so you're ready for the busy months ahead.

- [ ] **Add a layer of mulch to bare soil** – Cover any exposed beds or borders with a few handfuls of compost, bark or leaf mould. It conserves moisture, suppresses weeds and keeps soil life happy. Organic mulch also improves soil as it breaks down. (Any bags you get, don't forget to give them a 'Jonny slap' before using them – I'm not asking, I'm telling!)

20-MINUTE JOBS

Got a bit more time? These slightly longer jobs will keep things running smoothly and feel really satisfying when they're done.

- [ ] **Prune your roses and give them a mulch feed** – Grab your secateurs and shape up your roses by removing dead or crossing stems. Mulch around the base with compost or well-rotted manure to lock in moisture and feed the soil.

- [ ] **Rake and top-dress a flower bed** – Clear any fallen leaves or debris, then add a layer of compost or organic matter across the surface. Your plants will thank you with fresh growth.

- [ ] **Plant out hardy herbs** – Get your thyme, chives, parsley and mint (always in a pot!) into the ground or containers. These toughies handle spring chills and get going quickly.

- [ ] **Sow peas or broad beans in prepared trenches** – Dig shallow trenches, pop in your seeds, cover and water. You'll be harvesting delicious pods in just a few months.

- [ ] **Clean and organise your tool shed** – A tidy-up now saves time later. Wipe down surfaces, hang up tools and chuck anything rusty or broken into the recycling pile.

- [ ] **Start a compost heap, if you don't already have one** (using the handy guide on page 59) – Got a corner of the garden going unused? Stick a compost heap there. Chuck in your veg peelings, garden clippings and a few bits of cardboard, and boom – you're composting.

- [ ] **Set up a water butt for rain collection** – Connect it to a downpipe and let nature fill it for you. Free water is a win. It's also better for your plants than chlorinated tap water.

- [ ] **Plant up a hanging basket with spring flowers** – Use violas, primroses, trailing ivy and herbs like thyme. Hanging baskets are great space-savers and add instant cheer.

- [ ] **Divide overgrown clumps of snowdrops** – Once they've finished flowering, lift and gently divide the clumps, then replant them while they're still 'in the green'. It's the best way to spread them across your garden.

- [ ] **Create bee hotels or bug havens with leftover materials** – Drill holes in logs, bundle up bamboo canes, or stack some broken pots in a shady corner. These little spaces give helpful garden bugs a safe place to nest.

SPRING

 30-MINUTE JOBS

Half an hour? That's plenty of time to tackle a chunkier job that'll leave your garden looking better, feeling healthier and running more smoothly.

- ☐ **Clear a neglected border and replant with herbs or flowers** – Pull up weeds, dig in compost and get some new life in the ground. Try herbs like rosemary or flowers like echinacea for a low-fuss, high-reward refresh.

- ☐ **Construct supports for climbing beans or flowers** – Use canes, twine or even hazel branches to build wigwams or trellises. Get it done now before everything tangles up in itself.

- ☐ **Clean and reseed patchy areas of lawn** – Rake out any moss or thatch, sprinkle on grass seed and gently firm it down. Keep it moist and you'll have lush green coverage in a few weeks. Easy peasy!

- ☐ **Create labels for seedlings with upcycled materials** – Use lolly sticks, broken slate, or even old cutlery to mark what's growing where. It's a fun, crafty job with real purpose.

- ☐ **Lay a brick or stone path in veg beds to make access easier** – Create stepping stones or paths so you can weed and harvest without compacting the soil. It also makes your plot look lovely and tidy. Make sure the ground is level and the stepping stones are hammered firmly in place.

- ☐ **Start a mini wildlife pond with an old washing-up bowl or shallow bucket** – Dig it in, then add some stones, rainwater and a couple of oxygenating plants. You'll be amazed how quickly it attracts frogs, birds and insects.

- ☐ **Create a climber feature** – Fix a trellis to a fence or wall and get your climbers in now. Sweet peas will reward you with scent, colour and armfuls of cut flowers in early summer through to early autumn.

- ☐ **Paint or repair an old bench or garden structure** – Give your furniture or fencing a new lease of life with a fresh coat of paint or a few repairs. It's practical and you'll enjoy your space more when it looks cared for.

Spring Activities for Kids

Getting kids involved in the garden isn't just helpful, it's a brilliant way to spend time together and teach them about gardening. Spring is the perfect time to spark their curiosity, get their hands dirty and show them where real food (and fun!) comes from. Plus, it's a fantastic way to get them off screens and outside for a bit. Whether they're toddlers or teens, there's a way to get them stuck in. I have a chapter on this later on (see page 192), but here are a few of my tried-and-tested favourites:

Sow Seeds Together

Start with fast-growing, high-success seeds that give kids a sense of instant reward. Radishes, nugget-sized carrots, nasturtiums and peas are all excellent choices. The process of planting, watering and watching for that first little sprout is magical for kids.

Bonus: many of these can be eaten straight from the soil, which kids love (once you've given them a rinse, obviously).

Give them their own small pot, patch or seed tray and let them be in charge of it. Sure, it might go a bit wild, but that's part of the fun.

Have a Sunflower Competition

This is a firm favourite in our house. Every spring, we each plant a sunflower, and it's game on to see whose grows the tallest. The kids get fully into it, and I'm definitely not competitive at all. Honest. (I may have sabotaged my wife's sunflower... once...)

Sunflowers are brilliant because they grow fast, are hard to mess up, and look amazing. Plus, birds and bees love them. You can keep the challenge simple or go full leaderboard mode, complete with measuring sticks and name tags.

Create a Mini Fairy Garden or Dinosaur World

Take an old plant pot, fill it with soil or compost, and let your kids create a tiny world. Use pebbles for paths, little plants as trees, and moss for fairy lawns or dino forests. Add a few small toys or decorations like shells, sticks and painted rocks, and you've got a full afternoon of imaginative fun.

It's low-cost, creative, and gets them thinking about the natural world in a whole new way.

Spring is bursting with opportunities for connection, learning and memory-making. So hand them a trowel, let them wear mismatched wellies, and dive into the dirt together. My son loves gardening with me now and always wants to get involved – it's fantastic and reminds me of myself wanting to get stuck in when I was a kid.

My Final Thoughts on Spring Gardening

Spring can feel like a sprint, but it doesn't have to. You don't need to do it all at once, and you definitely don't need a garden centre's worth of products. What your garden needs is attention, patience and a bit of regular care. Whether you're carving out ten minutes with a cup of tea or diving in for a full thirty-minute blitz, these moments add up.

Gardening is as much about the process as it is about the results. Enjoy the fresh air, the scent of earth, the pleasure of watching something grow because you put your hands in the soil. You're not just tending plants, you're tending to yourself.

> I also encourage you to take photographs of your garden throughout the spring growing season. That way, at the end of the year, you can look back on the images, see what you liked (or didn't like) and plan for next year.

Grab your gloves and get stuck in. Spring is calling... and I know you're going to answer!

5
SUMMER
Keep It Alive (Without Watering 24/7)

Summer. It's the season that makes me both absolutely buzzing and slightly terrified as a gardener. Everything is in full swing, flowers exploding with colour, veg plots brimming with promise, bees working overtime, and yet, lurking in the background is the ever-present fear of heatwaves, drought and that moment when you realise your containers are bone dry because you forgot to water them for two days straight.

I love summer, truly. But let's not pretend it's all cocktails and sun hats. It's also the season when I've stood in my garden in absolute despair because my lawn has gone the colour of digestive biscuits, or because the tomatoes look like they've just come back from a fortnight in Tenerife and are refusing to perk up again.

In my garden in Warwickshire, summer is the season that tests me the most. We get weeks of glorious sunshine, then sudden torrential rain that flattens my dahlias. We've had entire Julys where I've barely had to water anything, and others where the hose has become a permanent fixture in my hand. Gardening in the UK in summer is unpredictable, and every year it teaches me something new.

I still remember the first summer in my own garden. I'd just bought my first house, and I was determined to grow all my own veg. I planted everything: tomatoes, courgettes, peppers, lettuce, and without any plan whatsoever. I watered the lot every day because I thought that's what good gardeners did. By July, I'd basically created a swamp. My courgettes were massive but tasteless, the tomatoes were dropping leaves from fungal disease, and my lawn looked like a patchy doormat. I learned the hard way that more water isn't always better, and that summer is just as much about restraint as enthusiasm.

One of my favourite things about summer is that it's the season when the mornings become magical. The sun's up early, the air is still cool and there's this

GARDEN YOURSELF HAPPY

incredible quiet before the chaos of the day starts. If you'd told 20-year-old me that I'd willingly be outside at 5.30am in my pyjamas, cup of tea in hand, pulling weeds and checking for aphids, I'd have laughed. But here we are.

It's in those early summer mornings that I feel most connected to the garden. The birds are singing, the bees are already at work, and the scent of damp earth is one of the best smells on the planet. That's when I spot things I'd miss otherwise, like the first runner bean flowers, or a sneaky outbreak of blackfly on the broad beans.

The other thing summer constantly reminds me of is that life doesn't stop just because the garden's going mad. I'm a firefighter, a husband, a parent, and I try to have something resembling a social life. I simply don't have endless hours to stand around with a watering can. Summer forces me to be smarter about how I garden.

I've learned that ten minutes here and there adds up. Some days, all I manage is a quick look around to spot what's wilting or pulling up a few weeds while the kettle boils. Other days, I might get a full hour to mow the lawn and tie in my sweet peas. It's all progress, and that's what counts.

I often say that gardening is like fitness training. As I'll keep reminding you, you're better off doing little and often than burning out in one go. Trust me, I've tried the all-day approach. My back still remembers digging an entire new bed in one sweaty August afternoon because I got 'inspired'. My wife remembers the moaning afterwards even more vividly. (And no, she wasn't overly sympathetic.)

I always think summer is for enjoying the garden. It's the season when the garden becomes an outdoor room. It's for evenings spent outside with friends, the smell of barbecues wafting through the air and the simple pleasure of picking herbs fresh for dinner.

Even when things go wrong (and they will), there's still so much joy to be had. The scent of lavender baking in the sun. The first ripe tomato off the vine.

The hum of bees bouncing from flower to flower. Those are the moments that keep me coming back, no matter how many times summer throws me a curveball.

So, in this chapter, I'll show you how to keep your garden alive, how to make smart choices that save water and time, and how to stay sane while doing it all. You don't need to become a slave to the hosepipe. You just need some know-how, and a willingness to adapt.

Let's get stuck in.

Watering in Depth: Smarter, Not Harder

If there's one thing summer makes us all obsessed with, it's watering. It's the season when your once-green lawn starts crunching underfoot, your pots seem to dry out the moment you turn your back, and every plant looks at you like you've personally betrayed it by not giving it a drink every five minutes.

I'll be honest, watering used to completely stress me out. My first summer gardening, I was out there every single evening, sloshing the hose around like a man possessed. The result? Waterlogged roots, fungal diseases and a water bill that made my eyes water. Lesson learned.

Here's what I know now: it's not about how often you water, it's about how well you water. So, let's dive into how to keep your garden thriving without tying yourself to a hosepipe.

WHY 'LITTLE AND OFTEN' DOESN'T WORK (FOR WATERING)

You've probably heard that phrase 'little and often' (I might've mentioned it a few times!). It's brilliant for weeding, pruning, or just pottering about. But for watering, it's the opposite of what you want. Okay, I know I've been going on and on (and on) about this throughout the book... and now I'm telling you to forget it?! But when it comes to watering, little and often just doesn't work – this is the one place you need to go big!

A light sprinkle every day barely penetrates the soil. Plants keep their roots close to the surface because that's where the moisture is. Then, when a heatwave hits, the top layer of soil dries out fast, and the plants suddenly have no reserves to draw from.

Instead, you want deep, thorough watering. You're aiming to soak the soil so that moisture sinks down to where roots can access it even after the surface dries out.

Here's my personal watering routine:
- **Timing:** I water either first thing in the morning or late in the evening. Early mornings are my favourite because it's cooler, and you avoid water sitting on leaves overnight, which can encourage mildew.
- **Method:** I use a watering can far more than a hose these days, especially on beds and borders. It forces me to be precise and stops me overwatering just because the hose is handy. Plus, it's more environmentally friendly when you're using water from a water butt.

- **Twice Round Rule:** I lightly water each section first, let it soak in for a couple of minutes, then go back over it for a deeper soak. It's amazing how much better the soil absorbs water this way.
- **Pots:** Containers dry out incredibly fast. I try to keep my pots grouped together in summer to create a humid microclimate. I also raise some pots slightly on bricks so water can drain properly.
- **Mulch:** After watering, I always add or fluff up mulch around the plants. It's one of the best ways to keep soil cool and moist for longer.

Here are a few more tricks I've picked up over the years:
- **Water slowly** – Rushing floods the surface but leaves dry soil underneath.
- **Use ollas or buried pots** – These clay pots release water slowly underground, a brilliant low-tech solution.
- **Re-use kitchen water** – Leftover water from rinsing veg (no soap!) is perfect for watering plants.
- **Shade your soil** – Planting densely or using ground covers reduces evaporation.

Watering in summer doesn't have to be a daily slog. With a few smart habits, you'll save water, time and a lot of stress. Trust me, there's nothing more satisfying than looking around a healthy garden, knowing you didn't waste half your summer attached to a hosepipe.

THE FINE ART OF PLANT HYDRATION

In my garden, I've noticed that my south-facing border near the patio dries out twice as fast as my side bed by the fence. That means I water them on completely different schedules. It sounds complicated, but over time you get to know your garden, and once you learn your garden's quirks, it becomes second nature to adjust depending on what they need.

It's also true that not every plant has the same natural thirst level. This is where knowing your garden really pays off. Of course, this will come with time, but here's a quick starter guide to common features that you can keep in mind.

Veggies
- **Salad crops**, such as lettuce and spinach, bolt quickly if they dry out. I keep these beds moist but never waterlogged.

- **Tomatoes, peppers, beans and aubergines** love consistent moisture but hate sitting in soggy soil. Water deeply at the base and avoid splashing the leaves.
- With **root vegetables**, such as carrots, radishes and parsnips, always water the soil at the base rather than the leaves. This allows the water to sink down to where the roots will be growing.

In my greenhouse, I've learned to water tomatoes in the morning rather than the evening. It reduces humidity and keeps blight at bay.

Lawns
Lawns look dramatic when they start turning brown, but they're surprisingly resilient. Mine goes brown every summer without fail and comes back as soon as the rain returns. Unless you're growing show turf, save yourself the stress and let your grass rest. More on this later in the chapter.

Flower Beds
- **Perennials** like echinacea, lavender and rudbeckia cope well with dry spells once established.
- **Hydrangeas**, however, are drama queens. Mine live in partial shade and still droop dramatically if I skip a watering session.
- **Dahlias** are one of my favourites but can be thirsty in the summer months – they love a good, deep soak.
- **Cosmos** (the annual varieties) are pretty easygoing and need a good water only a couple of times a week. Aim to keep the base moist and they'll flower all summer.

> One of my favourite garden investments was installing water butts. I've currently got two, and I'm eyeing up a third. Nothing feels better than knowing I'm watering my garden with rainwater, especially as summers become drier and, in the UK, hosepipe bans are understandably becoming more common. Rainwater is softer than tap water and better for acid-loving plants like blueberries and rhododendrons. Plus, it's free, which my wallet appreciates.

Planting and Summer Choices

One of my favourite things about summer is that the garden feels full of possibility. Everything's growing, there's colour everywhere, and you've still got time to sow, plant and tweak things as you go.

But here's the other truth: summer is also the time when plants can absolutely do your head in. One minute, they're thriving; the next, they're bolting to seed, wilting under blazing sun, or getting munched by every pest known to man.

Choosing what to grow and where makes all the difference. Let's talk about what's worked in my garden, what I've learned the hard way, and how to fill your space with plants that don't need babysitting 24/7.

You'd think the big planting season is spring. And it is. But summer planting is just as crucial. Why? Because:
- You can succession sow, so you keep harvesting fresh crops right into autumn.
- You can fill gaps where spring plants have gone over.
- Summer soil is warm, helping seeds germinate faster.
- You can still grow loads of flowers for late-season colour.

For years, I thought once summer hit, the planting ship had sailed. Turns out, summer is brilliant for keeping your garden vibrant, as long as you pick the right plants.

VEG TO SOW OR PLANT IN SUMMER

Let's start with the veg patch. Even in July or August, there's plenty you can sow or plant for late summer and autumn harvests.

Here's what's reliably good for me:
- **Salad Leaves** – Rocket, lettuce, mizuna – sow every couple of weeks and you'll have fresh salad all summer. In my garden, I grow these in pots right by the back door so I can grab a handful while making lunch.
- **Radishes** – So fast-growing, it's practically instant gratification. My kids love pulling them up.
- **Carrots** – Early summer sowings often bolt, but later sowings do brilliantly for autumn. Those with clay soil may prefer short-rooted types like 'Paris Market'.
- **Spring Onions** – Great for gaps between slower crops. Sow direct and thin out as you go.

- **Beetroot** – Quick-growing and brilliant roasted or grated into salads. Sow in July for tender autumn roots.

In my own garden, I try to keep some empty patches in spring ready for these summer sowings. They fill in the gaps and keep things productive. Plus, it's deeply satisfying to harvest fresh veg in September when everyone else thinks the season's finished.

FLOWERS TO SOW OR PLANT IN SUMMER

I absolutely love summer flowers. But not all flowers love summer. Some look spectacular for a week, then collapse into a crispy mess the second a heatwave hits. One summer, I planted a whole bed of pansies because they looked pretty in the garden centre. Terrible idea. By mid-July, they were a melted mess. Lesson learned, save pansies for cooler seasons.

These are my go-to summer survivors:
- **Zinnias** – Come in every colour imaginable and love heat. They're daisy-like flowers and really pretty.
- **Sunflowers** – I grow these every year with my kids and we have a family competition to grow the tallest sunflower.
- **Cosmos** – Tall, floaty stems topped with daisy-like flowers, these are easy, generous bloomers that are great in dry soil. If you consistently deadhead, they will keep on flowering. I grow mine from seed every year for a pop of bright pink.
- **Marigolds** – Bold, round flowers that come in a variety of colours, these are brilliant companion plants for the veg patch.
- **Verbena bonariensis** – Tall and airy with a slender stem topped with clusters of tiny purple flowers, these are drought-tolerant and a pollinator magnet.

HERBS TO SOW OR PLANT IN SUMMER

If there's one thing summer is perfect for, it's growing herbs. The heat brings out their oils and flavours beautifully.

My absolute favourites:
- **Basil** – Loves warmth but hates drying out. I grow mine in pots so I can move it into a bit of shade during heatwaves.
- **Thyme and Rosemary** – Mediterranean legends. Barely need watering once established.
- **Coriander** – Bolts fast in heat, so I sow a little every couple of weeks.
- **Mint** – Fantastic in summer drinks. Always grow in a pot, so it doesn't take over the garden.

A few years ago, I tried growing basil directly in my south-facing border. Within a week, the poor things were crispier than bacon rashers. Since then, they stay in pots near the kitchen where I can keep my eye on them. It also means you get a lovely scent that blows through when your windows or doors are open.

Above all, when choosing summer plants, I've learned this: **Choose plants that suit your conditions, not your wish list.**

It's so easy to fall in love with a plant at the garden centre, only to discover it's basically doomed in your specific garden. Trust me, I've been there. As I mentioned earlier, I once tried a whole bed of lupins because they looked brilliant on a TV gardening show. They were a total disaster in my heavy clay soil and rotted before midsummer.

Now, I grow what thrives, not just what looks pretty on a label. Summer gardening becomes much easier and much more fun when you work with the conditions of your garden rather than against them.

Summer is your chance to keep the garden productive, colourful and buzzing with life. Make good plant choices, adapt to changing weather and remember your garden should work for you, not the other way round.

Climate Change and Adapting Our Gardens

One of the biggest changes in summer gardening over the past decade has been climate change. When I was a kid, summer was reliably warm but temperatures were not extreme. Now, it can swing between scorching heatwaves and biblical rain. Plants that once thrived in British summers sometimes struggle, and droughts come round more often.

I've seen it in my own garden. My lawn used to go brown maybe one year in five, now it's nearly every summer unless I adjust how I care for it. Plants that would reliably sail through summer now wilt by June if I'm not careful. It has pushed me to rethink my planting, my watering habits, and how I plan for the future.

I remember the summer of 2022, when we hit 40°C in the UK. I'd never seen anything like it. My hydrangeas collapsed into sad, green puddles. The grass went brown and crunchy. Even some of my tough Mediterranean herbs started looking rough around the edges.

Climate change is shifting the gardening calendar, and the choices we make as gardeners are more important than ever. Here's what we're facing in British gardens (and across the world) now:

- **Hotter average temperatures** – More days above 25°C and more frequent heatwaves.
- **Longer dry spells** – Rainfall is less predictable, sometimes missing for weeks, then arriving all at once.
- **Sudden storms** – Intense rain can flood beds and wash away seeds or mulch.
- **Pests arriving earlier** – Warm winters mean aphids and other pests are active sooner and stick around for longer.

It sounds scary, but there's loads we can do to continue to protect our gardens and the wildlife that enjoy them. Gardeners are practical, resilient people (that should be our mantra!). We're used to dealing with unpredictable weather. We just need new strategies.

Here's how I'm changing things in my own patch, and how you might too:

1. CHOOSE DROUGHT-TOLERANT PLANTS

Every year, I swap a few more water-hungry plants for drought-tolerant species. Lavender, rosemary, echinacea and sedums are thriving in spots where my old English cottage favourites used to suffer and wilt. Plus, they bring pops of colour to the summer border. I'm especially fond of *verbena bonariensis*. Tall, elegant and barely needing a drink once established, it's become one of my summer must-haves.

2. MULCH MORE GENEROUSLY

I've always mulched (more on this later in the book), but these days I'm adding thicker layers than ever. A good 5–8cm of compost, bark chips or leaf mould around my plants locks in moisture and keeps roots cool.

In the heatwave of 2022, the only parts of my garden that didn't crack open like a dry biscuit were the mulched beds.

3. HARVEST RAINWATER

Rainwater harvesting has gone from a 'nice idea' to an 'absolute essential'. I've got two water butts connected to the house gutters and I'm looking at adding another this year. During last summer's dry spells, those butts saved my veg beds.

4. CREATE SHADE

You could try experimenting more with creating microclimates. For example:
- Growing climbers on pergolas to cast dappled shade below.
- Planting taller plants, like sunflowers or beans, to shield smaller crops.
- Using shade cloth in the greenhouse during the hottest weeks.

A few years ago, I'd never have considered 'shade planning' for summer. Now it's part of how I design the garden to keep it looking its best for longer.

5. IMPROVE SOIL HEALTH

Healthy soil holds water better and stays cooler. I'm obsessed with adding organic matter like well-rotted manure or garden compost. I also have a compost bin so that every bit of compost I make goes straight back into the garden. It's like giving your soil a gym membership. Even in dry spells, beds with good soil stay moist a few days longer than my old, more neglected borders.

6. ADJUST PLANTING TIMES

Some seeds just don't handle early summer heat anymore. I now stagger my sowings and sometimes push them into cooler months. For example:
- Sowing lettuce in partial shade rather than full sun.
- Delaying carrot sowings until after the hottest spells.
- Spinach does not geminate well in hot soil.
- Cabbage gets stressed if it's too hot, resulting in loose heads and pest problems.

It's all about working with the new rhythms rather than fighting them, and making sure you're keeping the joy in gardening.

One thing I refuse to let warmer summers steal is the joy I get from watching my flowers bloom and veg grow. Yes, it's getting trickier. But there's still so much beauty and satisfaction in coaxing things to grow, even in a hotter climate.

I remind myself that gardeners have always adapted. We're not giving up, we're just learning new tricks. And in some ways, I've found these changes make me even more connected to my garden. I pay closer attention and I'm more mindful of water, soil and how everything interacts.

Gardening in summer is changing but that doesn't mean it's over. It just means we keep growing smarter. And honestly? That's part of what makes gardening so fascinating in the first place. There's always space to learn.

Summer Lawn Care (and the Mistakes I've Made Along the Way)

As you know, I'm a bit of a lawn geek. There's just something about the smell of freshly cut grass, the satisfaction of crisp edges and those stripes glinting in the sun... It scratches a very particular itch in my brain. I go into lots more detail about prepping the perfect lawn in Chapter 8, but let me give you some summer tips here!

Summer is where lawns either shine or completely fall to pieces. Hot weather, dry spells, football games and barbecues all take their toll. And if you're like me, juggling work, family and the odd attempt at a social life, it's not always easy to give your grass the TLC it deserves.

Over the years, I've learned how to keep a lawn looking decent through summer without becoming a slave to the sprinkler. Here's how I manage my own patch, and how you can keep yours alive (and maybe even looking lush), even during the trickiest weeks of the year.

Let me tell you about my first summer as a homeowner. I was determined to have the perfect lawn. I mowed it every other day, watered it constantly and even bought a set of those fancy stripes rollers. By mid-July, it looked glorious... until the first heatwave hit. Overnight, it went from emerald green to a patchy, straw-coloured wasteland. My neighbour popped his head over the fence and said, 'Gave it a bit of a hammering, didn't you?' Ouch!

I'd cut it far too short and basically fried the roots. Lesson learned, longer grass handles heat better. If I could give you just one piece of summer lawn advice, it's this: raise your mower blades.

Aim to leave your grass around 5–7cm high during summer. Taller grass shades the soil, reducing water loss. It also helps crowd out weeds and moss.

Now I mow once a week during the summer (twice maximum if we've had rain) and I keep the cut gentle. No more scalping my lawn into oblivion.

WHETHER TO WATER IN SUMMER

Don't panic about brown patches. This one took me a while to accept – it's perfectly normal for a lawn to go brown in summer. It's the grass's way of protecting itself. It goes dormant, stops growing and saves its energy for when the rain comes back.

A question I get asked all the time is: 'Should I water my lawn in summer?' Here's my honest answer:

- No, not usually. Grass is surprisingly tough and will recover.
- Yes, if you're dealing with new turf, recently overseeded patches, or if you want show-quality turf.

If you do choose to water your lawn:

> Water deeply, once a week max.
> Early morning is best.
> Let water soak in rather than running off the surface.

Personally, unless I've got a new patch of grass establishing, I rarely water my lawn in summer anymore. I save the water for my veg beds, summer flowers and pots.

WHAT TO FEED YOUR LAWN IN SUMMER

Summer isn't the time for heavy feeding. Overfeeding during heat can stress the grass. Instead:

- Use a light, organic, summer lawn feed, if your grass looks tired.
- Avoid high-nitrogen fertilisers, which promote too much leafy growth.

I prefer seaweed-based feeds. They're gentle, improve soil health and help the grass cope with stress.

GIVING YOUR LAWN SPACE TO BREATHE

Another one of my favourite summer lawn secrets is aeration. (Again, I go into this in much more detail later on in the book, if you're not completely sure what to do – see page 147.)

Compacted soil is one reason grass struggles in heat. Aerating helps water and air get down to the roots. It sounds fancy, but all you need is a garden fork.

How to aerate using a garden fork:
- Stab the fork into your lawn every 10–15cm.
- Wiggle it slightly to open channels.
- Do this in early summer before heat peaks.

REPAIRING WORN PATCHES

Summer is when worn patches show up, whether caused by kids, pets or garden parties. A couple of years ago, we hosted a big family barbecue. By the end, the lawn looked like the aftermath of a music festival. The patch-repair routine saved me from a bald lawn for the rest of the summer, and it doesn't take long to give it that refresh.

Here's what I do:

> Loosen compacted soil with a fork.
> Sprinkle grass seed evenly.
> Lightly rake it in.
> Water gently.
> Keep the patch moist until new shoots appear.

MY SUMMER LAWN SCHEDULE

I know this all seems like a lot of information, so I've broken it down into my typical summer lawn schedule:
- **Weekly mow** – high setting, gentle trim.
- **Monthly edges** – keeps things looking sharp.
- **Aerate once or twice** – if we've had dry spells.
- **Keep an eye on patches** – repair as needed.
- **Enjoy it** – sit out with a cuppa and admire the stripes.

It really is as simple as that.

Summer lawn care doesn't have to be a battle. Raise your blades, avoid panic-watering and give your grass time to recover. The goal isn't a perfect green carpet, it's a healthy lawn that bounces back when summer's heat finally breaks.

And remember, it's also meant to be enjoyed. So, kick off your shoes, feel the grass between your toes and remind yourself why you love having a lawn in the first place.

Quick Jobs for Summer

Here's the brilliant thing about summer gardening: you don't need hours to make a difference. Between work, family and all the chaos life throws at us, sometimes you've only got ten minutes spare and that's fine. Just as we did in the previous chapter, let's have a look at what you can achieve in quick bursts of time. I've also included some insight into how I tackle these jobs in my own patch. Tick off the jobs as you go and enjoy that sense of achievement.

 10-MINUTE JOBS

Even ten minutes can transform your garden or at least stop it descending into chaos. Here's what I tackle when time's short in those summer months:

☐ **Deadhead flowers** – Nothing lifts a border like deadheading. I often grab a mug of tea and wander round snipping off spent blooms. This keeps plants flowering longer and stops them going to seed too soon. One summer morning, still in my pyjamas, I ended up deadheading half of my cosmos bed before the kettle boiled. Not glamorous, but it works.

☐ **Check containers** – Pots dry out fast in summer. I stick my finger into the compost – if it feels dry an inch down, it's time to water. My own patio pots are in full sun, so I group them together for shade and easier watering runs. It also looks great.

☐ **Tie in climbers** – Sweet peas, beans and clematis love a good wander. If you've got five minutes, gently tie in new shoots before they become an untamed jungle. I use garden string for this job.

☐ **Pest patrol** – Flip leaves over and look for aphids, whitefly or caterpillars. Squash small infestations before they become an army. I've learned the hard way, ignore blackfly for a week, and suddenly your broad beans look like they've joined a horror film. You can also use mild soap and water to clean them off.

- ☐ **Pull weeds** – A quick whip round with a hoe, or a hand-pull, keeps weeds from setting seed. I do this while chatting on the phone or waiting for dinner to cook. It's actually a job my wife quite enjoys too (bonus).

- ☐ **Sweep paths** – Keeps the garden looking tidy and stops algae building up.

- ☐ **Harvest herbs or salad leaves** – Even a small harvest feels like a win. I'm always pinching off basil, snipping rosemary, or grabbing a handful of rocket for sandwiches.

- ☐ **Tidy tools** – Brush off soil, wipe blades and hang things back where they belong. This saves headaches next time you're in a rush, and you'll save time looking for the tool you need.

- ☐ **Top up mulch** – A handful of mulch around thirsty plants buys you time in hot weather.

 ## 20-MINUTE JOBS

A spare 20 minutes is golden. Here's how you can get to work:

- ☐ **Prune perennials** – Cut back any perennials that have flopped or finished flowering. It tidies the bed and often encourages a fresh flush of growth. Last summer, my hardy geraniums started to take over. Twenty minutes later, the border was neater and the plants rebounded beautifully.

- ☐ **Plant up gaps** – Even in mid-summer, you can slot in quick annuals, such as cosmos or marigolds, for instant colour. I keep a tray of emergency plants behind the shed, ready to fill gaps where something's died or been eaten. I love cosmos. I grow them from seed every year, so always have some to hand.

SUMMER

- [ ] **Deep water your beds** – Instead of rushing with a hose every day, spend 20 minutes soaking a key bed properly. Your plants will thank you for it.

- [ ] **Sow fast-growing crops** – Things like radishes, salad leaves or dwarf beans still do well if sown in summer warmth.

- [ ] **Repair supports** – If your climbers are flopping or canes have snapped, take time to fix them now before plants are too heavy to move.

- [ ] **Make a bee hotel** – Bundle hollow stems (like bamboo) into a tin can or wooden box. It's perfect for solitary bees. My kids love helping to make these and checking who's moved in. We have several dotted around the garden.

- [ ] **Refresh compost in pots** – Scrape away the top few centimetres of compost, replace with fresh compost, then water in. Instant boost for your blooms.

- [ ] **Thin fruit** – Apples, plums and pears often grow more fruit than they can handle. Thin them out so the remaining ones grow bigger and are tastier.

- [ ] **Clean the greenhouse** – Remove dead leaves, wipe glass to maximise light and check for pests lurking in corners.

- [ ] **Divide perennials** – Some perennials, like daylilies or irises, can get overcrowded. Summer is a good time to split them and replant.

 30-MINUTE JOBS

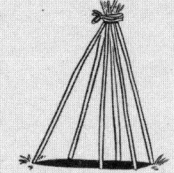

Half an hour is a luxury. Here's what I'd tackle:

- ☐ **Create a new planting area** – Clear a small patch, add compost and plant up with summer bedding or herbs.

- ☐ **Build supports for beans** – There's something satisfying about building a wigwam of canes and tying it together. My kids once asked if I was constructing a giant tipi. Also fun and satisfying.

- ☐ **Re-pot large containers** – Check roots, add fresh compost and water thoroughly. Summer is prime time for a container refreshment.

- ☐ **Deep clean bird baths** – Birds suffer in heat. Scrub out algae and refill with fresh water.

- ☐ **Light pruning** – Prune summer-flowering shrubs *after* blooms fade. This keeps them tidy and encourages growth next year.

- ☐ **Tidy the shed** – I try to do this once a season. It never stays tidy for long, but for one brief, shining moment, I know where everything is and there are fewer huge spiders in there.

- ☐ **Start a water butt project** – Install a rainwater barrel or extend existing guttering. It's one of the best long-term drought solutions.

- ☐ **Build a bug hotel** – Use old wood, bricks, hollow stems and pine cones. A brilliant way to add wildlife interest and something the whole family can get involved in.

- ☐ **Refresh mulch across borders** – Spread a fresh layer across beds for moisture retention and weed suppression.

- ☐ **Check greenhouse crops** – Pinch out tomato side shoots, tie in cucumbers and look for early signs of blight or pests.

My Final Thoughts on Summer Gardening

If I've learned anything over the years, it's that summer is a season of extremes and surprises. Some days you'll feel like the king or queen of your garden, with everything flowering and thriving. Other days, you'll stand there staring at wilted hydrangeas or frazzled lawns, wondering what on earth went wrong.

But that's gardening. It's never perfect. It's messy, unpredictable and sometimes frustrating. Yet it's also one of the most rewarding things you'll ever do.

Remember, your garden doesn't need perfection. It needs you. Your presence. Your care. Your time, even if it's only five minutes snipping off dead flowers before work. Little and often wins. Summer gardening is a marathon, not a sprint. Ten minutes one evening, twenty the next morning, it all adds up. Sometimes the best thing you can do for your garden is simply to sit down with a brew and admire how far you've come.

One of my favourite summer rituals is sitting in the garden late in the evening. The kids are in bed, the sun's setting, and there's that magical hum of insects and the scent of warm earth. It's moments like that when I'm reminded why I garden at all. It's not just about the plants, it's about the peace, the connection and the chance to breathe.

> Remember to take photographs of your garden throughout the summer and store them with your spring photographs. At the end of the year, you can look back on the images, see what you liked (or didn't like) and make a plan for next year.

So, enjoy your summer garden. Water wisely, plant cleverly, and above all, give yourself permission to relax and soak it all in. Your garden and your mind will thank you for it.

6
AUTUMN
Prepping for Next Year

Autumn is the season when a lot of people throw in the towel (or trowel?) on gardening. The evenings get damp, the nights draw in and that lush summer display of flowers starts fading fast. The barbecue's packed away, the lawn chairs are shoved into the shed and suddenly the garden feels a little less exciting. But here's the thing, autumn isn't the end of the gardening year, it's where you press the reset button.

This is the season where you quietly prepare your garden for its long winter nap, and – perhaps more importantly – set the stage for next spring. Think of it as wrapping the garden up in a blanket, whispering 'sleep well' and secretly leaving presents under the tree for yourself to open next year. Every bulb planted, every pile of leaves cleared, every perennial divided, it's all future joy in the making.

I get why people back off in autumn. The weather's unpredictable, the evenings are darker and it's very tempting to stay inside with a brew (or something stronger) instead of wrestling with soggy leaves. But if you can push yourself out there, even for ten minutes, you'll reap the rewards later. Autumn isn't about doing everything in one back-breaking weekend. It's about small, steady steps that make your life easier come spring.

For me, autumn has always felt like a calmer season in the garden. Summer can be chaos if you don't break your tasks down. Mowing weekly, watering daily, deadheading endlessly, chasing after plants that are growing like they're on steroids. Autumn slows that all down. The work shifts from maintenance to preparation. It's less about keeping up and more about quietly getting ahead. After a full-on shift at the fire station, there's nothing I love more than stepping into the garden on a crisp autumn evening, rake in hand, mist hanging in the air, and that earthy smell of damp leaves filling my nose. It feels like the garden and I are both exhaling.

And there's something about autumn light, golden, softer, wrapping everything in a glow that makes even the mess look good. It might be my second favourite season. It's quieter, more reflective, less frantic. And when life feels busy and heavy, I need that kind of season to remind me to slow down.

So why bother? Why not just let nature get on with it and worry about things in spring? Because what you do now makes spring gardening about ten times easier. Skip autumn jobs, and you'll spend the first warm weekend of March knee-deep in weeds, battling mossy lawns and realising you forgot to plant bulbs (rookie error – yes, I've done it). Do a little prep now, and your future self will be smugly sipping tea in April while everyone else is panicking.

Why Autumn Matters
- **The soil's still warm.** Roots keep growing even when the air cools. Anything you plant now – bulbs, shrubs, perennials – gets a head start.
- **There's more rain.** Summer dries everything out, but autumn brings back moisture. Perfect for helping new plants settle.
- **Weeds slow down.** You can win the battle for once. Clear them now, and they won't come back as quickly.
- **Less pressure.** The big summer display is done. You can potter at your own pace without feeling like you're always behind.
- **Wildlife needs you.** Autumn is when hedgehogs, birds and bugs are all looking for food or a cosy place to hibernate. A few simple jobs can make your garden a haven.

For me, autumn gardening is all about optimism. Every bulb I bury is a little promise to myself that spring will come back around. Every bag of leaves I clear is a reminder that the garden is still alive, even as it looks like it's going to sleep. It's the season of letting go (cutting back, clearing away), preparing for rest and trusting that growth will come again. You don't have to do everything perfectly – dead plants happen, bulbs sometimes rot and leaves will keep falling no matter how many times you rake them up! The point isn't perfection, it's participation.

So, kettle on, gloves out, and let's get into the rhythm of autumn. In this chapter, we'll aim to tick off the essential jobs and set yourself up for a calmer, smoother spring. And you might even find, like me, that autumn becomes one of your favourite seasons to be in the garden.

Leaf Management

Let's start with the most obvious autumn job: dealing with leaves.

Now, don't get me wrong, I love leaves and have been known to rake them in a pile, then throw them up in the air while playing with the kids. I love the colours, the crunch and that feeling of walking through a carpet of gold and russet. However, left alone, leaves can smother lawns, clog drains and turn patios into an ice rink. So, leaf management isn't about fighting autumn, it's about working with it.

Here are some tips:

- **On the lawn** – This is the big one. Leaves block sunlight and trap moisture. If you leave them lying there, you'll end up with bald patches and moss. I rake mine every week or so, depending on how many leaves are falling. It doesn't have to be perfect or too time-consuming, just enough to let the grass breathe.
- **In borders** – Here you can relax. Leaves are free mulch (more on that later). Let them sit, and they'll break down, feeding the soil. The only rule is don't let a massive soggy blanket bury your smaller plants. Delicate perennials will suffocate if they're completely covered.
- **On patios and paths** – Sweep them off before they get slimy. Trust me, nothing kills your gardening dignity faster than going flat on your backside because of a wet leaf.
- **Compost them** – We touched on this in the Spring chapter. You could add them to your compost heap or bag them up in black bin liners, poke a few holes in the sides, then tuck them away in a corner. In 12–18 months, you'll have leaf mould, an amazing free soil conditioner. Garden centres charge good money for this stuff, so why not make your own?

Don't stress about being perfect. You don't need to chase every single leaf with military precision. Just keep on top of it, bit by bit, and you'll protect your lawn, keep paths safe and make some compost gold for later.

Mulching: Feeding the Soil

Now, let's briefly talk about mulching, probably one of the most misunderstood garden jobs. I promise, it's not complicated. In fact, it might be the single easiest way to improve your soil and plants. There's lots more information later in the book, but it's such a key job for the autumn months, I've covered the basics here.

So, what is mulch? Simply put, mulch is a blanket for your soil. It's a layer of organic matter (like compost, bark, leaf mould, or well-rotted manure) spread on top of the soil. You're not digging it in; you're just laying it down.

Three big reasons to mulch:
1. **It protects the soil.** Rain and frost can compact bare soil. Mulch helps keep it loose and healthy.
2. **It feeds your plants.** As the mulch breaks down, it adds nutrients back into the soil. Think of it as slow-release plant food.
3. **It keeps weeds down.** Cover bare soil, and weeds find it harder to germinate. That means less weeding for you next year (you're welcome).

HOW TO MULCH (BASIC LEVEL)

I usually mulch in October, once the borders are tidied. There's something satisfying about it, and it instantly makes the garden look neat and tidy. Plus, you know you're setting everything up for an easier spring.

1. **Weed first.** There's no point mulching over weeds; they'll just laugh and grow through.
2. **Choose your mulch.** Use compost, bark chippings, leaf mould, or even straw if you're mulching veg beds.
3. **Spread a 5cm layer.** Not too thin, or it won't work; not too thick, or plants suffocate.
4. **Keep away from stems.** Don't pile mulch right against plant bases, as it can cause rot.

Also, don't overthink it. You don't need perfect compost or fancy bark chips. Use what you've got. Even a thin scatter of homemade compost makes a difference. And if you've got heavy clay soil (like me), mulching every year is non-negotiable. It stops your garden turning into a swampy mess in winter.

Seed Saving: Nature's Freebie

Autumn is hands-down the best time for seed saving. Seed saving is when you collect seeds from the plants you've already grown. Plants have done their thing all summer, and now they're winding down, producing seed heads, pods and capsules. For gardeners, this is like finding free money lying around your borders (maybe not quite as exciting, but close). Why buy seed packets every year when your own plants will happily provide you with next year's crop?! There's a step-by-step guide coming up, so don't worry if you've not done this before.

The best bit? You don't need fancy kit. Just some paper envelopes, a pen and maybe a dry afternoon.

Why Save Seeds?

- **It saves money.** This is an obvious one. Why pay pounds per packet when you've got 200 seeds sitting in your flower bed?
- **It gives you more plants.** You can fill borders, pots, and even give extras to friends and family.
- **It keeps the cycle going.** There's something deeply satisfying about sowing seeds that you collected yourself and watching them grow the following year.
- **It feels old-school.** Gardeners have been saving seeds for thousands of years. You're part of a tradition and it's hugely satisfying.

WHAT TO SAVE

If you're new, stick with the simple ones first:
- **Sunflowers** – Let the heads dry on the plant. Once they go brown, rub out the seeds with your thumb. Easy. If you have excess sunflower seeds, the birds love them too.
- **Marigolds (*Calendula*)** – Those curly, claw-like seeds are ready once the petals have started to fall off and the flower head is brown. They should feel dry and firm.
- **Sweet peas** – Leave some of the blooms and allow them to turn into seed pods. They'll go dry and will rattle – that's when it's time to pick them.
- **Beans and peas** – Same method as sweet peas.
- ***Nigella* (Love-in-a-Mist)** – Let the flowers fade naturally and wait until they turn brown and papery. They should feel dry and hard to the touch.

HOW TO SAVE SEEDS

1. **Pick your seeds from strong, healthy plants.** This will help ensure the next lot of plants grows well, as they've already had a good start!
2. **Pick the right time.** Wait until seed heads or pods are completely dry and brown. Damp seeds = mouldy disaster.
3. **Collect carefully.** On a dry day, snip the pods/heads into a paper bag, then gently shake out the seeds from the seed pods.
4. **Dry the seeds.** Spread out your seeds on a paper towel and keep in a cool, dry place for a few days until completely dry. Remove any bits of fluff or plant material (unless you like surprises). Don't forget to admire your handiwork!
5. **Label.** Trust me, you won't remember what they all are, so labelling is key. Write down the plant name and date you harvested them.
6. **Store.** Paper envelopes are best (plastic sweats and causes rot). Keep them somewhere cool and dry.

If in doubt, just try it. Even if half your seeds don't germinate, you'll still have more than enough. Plus, they make lovely gifts for friends and family. They should save well for the year if kept in the right conditions.

I still remember the first time I saved sunflower seeds. I felt like some kind of survivalist genius. 'Look at me! I've harvested my very own stash of seeds!' Then, the next spring, when those first seedlings popped up, I was hooked. It's not just about saving money; it's about closing the loop in your garden.

Bulb Planting: Hope in a Packet

Now we get to my absolute favourite autumn job: planting bulbs. Honestly, if you only do one thing this autumn, make it bulbs.

Why? Because bulbs are little parcels of joy. You dig a hole, drop them in, cover them up and forget about them. Then, just when you're convinced winter will never end, bam! Crocuses, daffodils, tulips. It's like a firework show, but quieter, cheaper and less stressful for the pets.

I plant so many bulbs over the autumn that I forget what I've done. It's always a nice surprise seeing what pops up where. Plus, we have a cheeky squirrel (we've called him Steven) that likes to dig them up and move them, too!

A bulb is basically a plant's energy storage unit. Inside that papery package is everything it needs to sprout when the conditions are right. You don't need to feed it, you don't need to water it all winter – you just plant it and it does its thing. For beginners, it doesn't get easier.

 ## WHEN TO PLANT SPRING-FLOWERING BULBS

September/October: Daffodils, crocuses, hyacinths, alliums.
October/November: Tulips (plant later to avoid 'tulip fire' disease).

If you're a bit behind, don't panic. I've planted tulips in December before and they still came up. Plants want to grow, you just have to give them the chance.

HOW TO PLANT BULBS

1. **Pick your spot.** Most bulbs like well-drained soil and a good amount of sun.
2. **Dig a hole.** Rule of thumb: three times the bulb's height. So, a 5cm crocus bulb = 15cm hole.
3. **Position.** Pointy end pointing up, flat end down. (If you really can't tell, plant sideways, plants are clever and will sort themselves out.)
4. **Cover and firm.** Gently replace the soil and press it down. Don't stamp, just enough to stop air gaps.
5. **Water in.** If the soil's already damp, you can skip this. But otherwise, a light sprinkle with the watering can will do.

Top tip: Plant bulbs in groups, not single lines, and experiment with planting different varieties together. Scatter a handful on the ground, then plant them where they land. It'll look more natural and less like you've tried to form a daffodil army.

MY MUST-HAVE BULBS FOR BEGINNERS

- **Daffodils**: Tough as nails. Plant and forget. They'll come back every year and give you that first sign of spring when they start poking through with their sunny yellow flowers.
- **Tulips**: Gorgeous, but a bit fussier, there is a huge variety of tulips to choose from. Treat as an annual, as they don't reflower well.
- **Crocuses**: The first splash of colour in late winter, with colours of purple, yellow or white. These small flowers bloom close to the ground and are great for lawns and pots.
- **Alliums**: Giant purple pom-poms in early summer. Bees love them and they are my absolute favourite. I'm slightly obsessed.
- **Hyacinths**: Incredible scent, pretty bell-shaped flowers, these make great additions, especially near doors or windows.

Planting bulbs isn't just about flowers. It's about **hope**. It's about giving yourself a reason to look forward to spring. When it's dark at 4pm in January, knowing you've got tulips waiting under the soil is a real mood booster.

And honestly? Bulb planting is one of those jobs where you get maximum reward for minimum effort. Ten minutes with a trowel in October can give you weeks of colour in April. That's gardening at its finest.

Your Garden Reset

By autumn, a lot of the garden looks... well, a bit knackered. Flowers that were dazzling in July now look like they've been through a washing machine. Leaves flop, stalks go brown and you might be tempted to rip the whole lot out and start fresh next year. But hold fire, this stage is actually crucial. If you know what to cut back, what to leave and what to divide, you'll set your garden up beautifully for spring. And if you grow veg or fruit, autumn is your moment to enjoy the spoils.

Cutting back, dividing and harvesting are all about **resetting**. You're giving your plants a fresh start, multiplying what you've got and enjoying the final rewards of the season. For beginners, it might feel intimidating ('What if I cut too much?'), but honestly, plants are resilient. They want to grow. And the more you interact with them, the more you'll learn their rhythms.

Cutting Back

Think of cutting back as giving your plants a seasonal trim. You're not killing them, you're just tidying up the bits they don't need. There are several benefits to this:

- **Prevents rot.** Some plants collapse into a soggy mess after frost and leaving them smothering the soil can spread disease.
- **Keeps things neat.** A trimmed border looks calmer and cared-for.
- **Encourages regrowth.** Cutting back lets the plant focus on its roots, ready for a burst of energy in spring.

WHAT TO CUT BACK IN AUTUMN

- **Hostas, peonies, phlox, daylilies** – These turn mushy. Chop them to ground level once the leaves have yellowed. It looks drastic, but they'll come back thriving next year.
- **Lavender** – Trim back after it's finished flowering in early autumn. Cut off the the faded flower stems and about a third of the soft green growth to keep a tidy shape in a rounded mound.
- **Herbaceous perennials** (plants that die back fully each year) – If the stems are black and flopping, it's safe to cut them down.

Don't panic about precision. Use sharp secateurs, cut the stems close to the base and remove dead leaves. Plants are tougher than you think.

WHAT NOT TO CUT BACK

- **Grasses** (like miscanthus, stipa, pennisetum). They look amazing frosted in winter light, almost magical.
- **Seed heads** (like echinacea, rudbeckia, sedum). Birds will feed on them, and they add structure to your border.
- **Shrubs**. Most shrubs don't want a haircut until late winter or spring, so let them alone a little longer.

Think of it this way: if it looks interesting, is standing upright, or useful to wildlife, leave it. If it looks like a puddle of slime or a floppy mess, chop it.

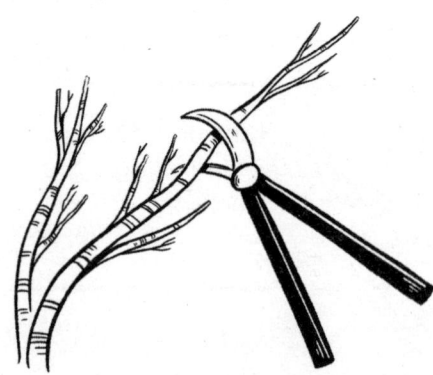

Dividing Perennials

This is one of gardening's best-kept secrets. A perennial is a plant that comes back year after year. Over time, some get too big for their boots, crowding themselves out or leaving a bald patch in the middle. Dividing them in early autumn not only keeps them healthy but also gives you free plants.

Why Divide?
- Stops overcrowding and improves flowering.
- Rejuvenates tired plants.
- Creates new plants for free (and who doesn't love freebies?).

HOW TO DIVIDE

1. **Choose your plant.** Look for clumps with a bald centre or ones that have clearly outgrown their spot. Hardy geraniums, daylilies and hostas are great starters if you've not done this before.
2. **Dig it up.** Use a fork or spade to lift the whole plant clump from the soil. Don't be shy, it can take a bit of muscle, but try to keep the root system intact.
3. **Split it.** Shake off excess soil so you can clearly see the roots and use a sharp spade, old bread knife, or even your hands to separate the clump into chunks. Each chunk should have roots and shoots. Remove any tired parts of the plant at this stage.
4. **Replant.** Put one clump back where the old plant was and plant the extras elsewhere or gift them. Water well and keep the soil moist until the roots establish.

You're basically cutting one big cake into slices. As long as each slice has some root and leaf, it'll grow.
I still remember the first time I divided a hosta. I was nervous and convinced I'd kill it. Fast-forward to the next spring and not only did it survive, it came back twice as lush. Plus, I had two extra clumps for free. It felt a bit like magic.

Harvesting: The Best Part of Gardening

If you grow fruit or veg, autumn is when it all pays off. Even if you don't, chances are you'll still have something to pick. Apples, berries, or maybe a stray squash that crept into your border.

WHAT TO HARVEST IN AUTUMN

- **Veg** – Pumpkins, squashes, carrots, parsnips, beetroot, kale, leeks.
- **Fruit** – Apples, pears, blackberries, late raspberries.
- **Herbs** – Parsley, thyme, rosemary.

BEGINNER TIPS FOR HARVESTING

- **Don't wait too long.** Pumpkins and squashes should be harvested before hard frost. Check for a tough rind and a hollow sound when tapped.
- **Twist, don't tug.** Apples and pears are ready if they come away with a gentle twist. If you're yanking, they're not ripe and need a little longer.
- **Use what you can; store the rest.** Carrots and parsnips can stay in the ground, but apples need storing in a cool place.

There's something primal about harvesting. Pulling a parsnip from frosty soil or carrying a basket of apples inside makes you feel connected to the land in a way supermarket shopping never can. And pumpkins? They're the poster child of autumn gardening. Grow them, carve them, roast them, they just scream 'autumn'.

Cleaning Greenhouses and Pots

Autumn isn't just about plants; it's about the whole garden ecosystem. Once the last flowers fade, it's tempting to lock the shed and hibernate until spring. But here's the thing: pests and diseases don't take the winter off. They'll happily lurk in your greenhouse, pots and soil, waiting to ambush your plants next year.

Cleaning might not feel as glamorous as bulb planting or harvesting pumpkins, but it's the behind-the-scenes work that keeps a garden balanced and makes your life easier in the long run.

CLEANING GREENHOUSES

If your greenhouse is anything like mine, by autumn it looks like the aftermath of a student party. Empty compost bags, dusty pots, wilted tomato plants clinging to strings, and the odd snail hiding in a corner. It's chaotic, but it's also a paradise for pests if you leave it like that.

Why Clean in Autumn?

- **Provide more light.** Winter days are short enough and dirty glass cuts light even further.
- **Pest control.** Aphids, whitefly, red spider mites – they all love hiding in warm corners.
- **Disease prevention.** Old plant debris is like leaving a buffet out for moulds and fungi.
- **Mental reset.** Walking into a clean greenhouse in February is like opening a brand-new notebook, fresh and full of promise.

Step-by-Step Greenhouse Deep Clean

1. **Clear it out.** Remove everything: plants, pots, tools. Yes, it feels like moving house, but it's worth it. Tackle it bit by bit, if you're short on time.
2. **Sweep up debris.** Old compost, dead leaves, rogue tomato skins – put the lot in the green bin. Don't compost diseased material.
3. **Wash the glass.** Use warm, soapy water with a sponge or soft brush. Clean inside and out, so the maximum amount of light can get in.
4. **Scrub surfaces.** Benches, shelves, staging – wipe them down with a natural cleaner.

5. **Check corners.** Spiders are fine (I leave them, not because I'm scared though...), but hunt out slugs, snails or whitefly.

6. **Organise tools.** Clean and sharpen secateurs, neatly stack pots and coil hoses properly.

Don't overcomplicate it. You're basically giving your greenhouse a spring clean, just six months early.

I'll be honest, this is not my favourite job. But nothing beats the smug feeling in spring when you slide open a spotless greenhouse door, ready to sow seeds in a fresh, clean space.

CLEANING POTS AND TRAYS

Pots and seed trays are sneaky culprits for spreading disease. That black plastic pot that held a diseased geranium this year? If you reuse it without washing, it might pass problems on to next year's plants.

How to Clean Pots (the Simple Way)

1. **Empty them.** Chuck old compost on the compost heap or soil (unless there are any signs of disease).
2. **Wash.** Fill a bucket with hot, soapy water. Dunk pots and scrub with a brush or sponge.
3. **Rinse.** Clean water to wash off soap.
4. **Dry.** Leave them to air dry. I tend to stack them upside down to drain.

Don't worry if your pots aren't spotless. The goal is to get rid of dirt, mould and eggs from pests.

If you're working with trays or modules, give them the same treatment. Future you will thank you when your spring seedlings are thriving instead of mysteriously dying off.

Wildlife Care: Your Autumn Guests

Autumn is a brilliant time to give the wildlife that shares your garden a helping hand. Hedgehogs, frogs, birds and insects are all preparing for the cold months, just like we are. A little bit of effort from you now can make your garden a proper sanctuary.

Your garden doesn't shut down in autumn, it just changes who it's catering for. As plants slow down, animals start looking for shelter and food. If you help them now, they'll repay you by keeping pests down and filling your garden with life in spring.

HEDGEHOGS: THE GARDEN'S PEST PATROL

Hedgehogs eat slugs and snails like they're going out of fashion. If you want fewer holes in your hostas next year, give hedgehogs somewhere safe to sleep. We have had one in the garden for a few years now – the kids have called him Sonic, and we love watching him waddle across the lawn of an evening!

Here are some quick tips for attracting them:

- **Log piles:** Stack logs, sticks and leaves in a quiet corner where they won't be disturbed.
- **Hedgehog houses:** You can buy one or DIY one. Use untreated wood for the walls and straw or dry leaves for bedding. Make sure any edges are fairly smooth and pop on a roof. Make sure it's secure.
- **Access:** Cut a small hole in your fence (13cm x 13cm) so they can travel between gardens. Best check with your neighbour for this one!

INSECTS

Not all insects are baddies. Ladybirds, lacewings and solitary bees are brilliant for gardens. Encourage them by providing a safe habitat – a bug hotel:

- **DIY bug hotel:** Bundle sticks, hollow bamboo, pinecones and bricks with holes into a box or old crate.
- **Location:** Place it in a quiet, sheltered spot out of strong wind.

BIRDS

I love birds in the garden – they eat caterpillars, aphids and weed seeds. However, their food is scarcer in autumn and winter. Here are a few things you can do to help them:

- **Feeders:** Keep them clean and topped up with seeds, peanuts or fat balls.
- **Water:** Put out a shallow dish for drinking and bathing.
- **Nesting boxes:** Autumn is a great time to install them ready for spring.

If, like me, you have cats, make sure anything you pop out for the birds is placed high up enough, so the cats can't reach it.

FROGS, TOADS AND FRIENDS

If you've got a pond, don't fish out every leaf. A few will break down and provide shelter for amphibians. You can also leave a pile of rocks or logs near water for hibernation spots.

Helping wildlife makes your garden healthier, richer and more alive. For me, this part of autumn gardening ties everything together. It's a reminder that the garden isn't just about me, it's about all the creatures that share the space. Knowing a hedgehog might be snoozing in my log pile or that robins are queuing up at the feeder brings so much joy, even in the quiet months.

A Quick Word on Lawn Care

Now, I promised I wouldn't go too heavy on lawns here, because later in the book there's a whole chapter dedicated to them (trust me, I'll geek out properly then). But autumn is honestly the golden season for lawn care.

Why? Because the conditions are just right:

- The soil is still warm enough for grass seed to germinate.
- There's usually more rain (so less faff with watering).
- Growth is slowing down but not stopped, so grass has time to repair before winter.

Think of autumn as a spa break for your lawn. You're basically giving it a facial, a massage and a healthy smoothie before it goes into hibernation. If you skip it, you'll roll into spring with a patchy, muddy mess.

Step 1: Rake Out Thatch and Moss

If you've ever run your fingers through your hair and pulled out a clump of knots, that's basically what your lawn needs. Over summer, lawns collect 'thatch' (a mix of old grass, roots and debris), plus moss in shady areas. Left alone, this layer suffocates your lawn.

- Grab a **spring-tine rake** (the bendy metal one, not the flat-headed soil rake).
- Work across the lawn with short, firm strokes.
- You'll pull up scary amounts of brown thatch and moss. Don't panic – that's the point.

Step 2: Aerate (Give it Some Air)

Compacted soil is the enemy of healthy lawns. Over summer, kids, dogs and barbecue parties squash the ground solid. Roots can't breathe and water just sits on the surface. Aeration fixes this.

- The simplest way: use a **garden fork**. Stick it in the ground every 10–15cm, wiggle it a bit, then pull it out. Yes, it's a workout.
- Fancy way: **hollow-tine aerator** (removes plugs of soil for better airflow). This lets oxygen, water and nutrients get down to the roots where they're actually useful.

Step 3: Overseed Bare Patches

Got bald spots? (No judgment – lawns go bald just like the best of us.) Overseeding in autumn is the cure.

- Buy a general-purpose grass seed mix.
- Rake the soil lightly so the seed makes contact.
- Scatter seed evenly.
- Gently rake over and water in, if the ground's dry.

Within a few weeks, you'll see new shoots poking through, and by spring the bald patch will have blended in.

Step 4: Feed the Lawn

Here's where most beginners trip up: you can't just use any old lawn feed. Spring/summer feeds are high in nitrogen, which makes grass grow lush and green, but that's the last thing you want going into winter. In autumn, you need a feed that's:

- **Low in nitrogen** (so growth slows).
- **High in potassium** (strengthens roots and improves cold resistance).

It's like switching your diet from energy drinks to hearty soups. The lawn doesn't need a growth spurt, it needs resilience.

Step 5: Mow (But Lower)

Don't put the mower away just yet. Grass still grows slowly in autumn. Keep mowing until growth really stops (usually late October/early November).

- Drop the mower blades to a lower setting (about 4–5cm).
- Long enough to protect the soil, short enough not to flop over.

And yes, keep collecting the clippings, don't leave them lying around to form a soggy blanket.

Autumn lawn care isn't glamorous. You won't get Instagrammable before-and-afters in 24 hours. But it is one of those 'thank me later' jobs. Do a bit of raking, aerating, overseeding and feeding now, then when spring rolls around, you'll step out onto a lawn that looks smugly healthy while your neighbour's patch is sulking.

I'll go into much more detail in the Lawn Care chapter later, but for now: think of autumn as your chance to reset the grass and send it into winter fighting fit.

Quick Jobs for Autumn

Not everyone has whole weekends to spend in the garden. Life gets busy, evenings get dark. Sometimes you just want to pop outside with a cuppa, or a pumpkin-spiced latte, and 'do a thing' without breaking your back. That's why I love my 10-minute, 20-minute and 30-minute jobs. They're bite-sized tasks that make a real difference. Perfect if you're a beginner or short on time.

 10-MINUTE JOBS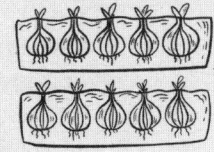

Here are some things you can get to when you're short on time.

- ☐ **Rake a small patch of leaves** – Rake a small section or gather a quick pile. Bag them for leaf mould (see page 89) or shove them in a wildlife corner. Even a tiny dent keeps your lawn breathing and stops slippery paths.

- ☐ **Check and clean a bird feeder** – Birds rely on us more in autumn. In ten minutes, you can refill a feeder with fresh seed and give the bird bath a quick scrub in hot, soapy water.

- ☐ **Plant a handful of bulbs** – Ten minutes = ten bulbs in the ground. Honestly, that's it. Use a bulb planter or just a trowel. Do a few every day, and by the end of autumn you'll have tucked away hundreds without ever feeling overwhelmed.

- ☐ **Deadhead stragglers** – Still got a few roses, dahlias or late bloomers hanging on? Snip off spent flowers just above a healthy set of leaves.

- ☐ **Sweep a path or patio** – It sounds boring, but sweeping leaves and mud off paths and paving makes the whole garden feel cared for. More importantly, it stops you (or the kids) going flying on a slippery bit of moss.

AUTUMN

 20-MINUTE JOBS

Got a bit more time and have a cuppa to hand? Get on with these 20-minute tasks that will leave you feeling a sense of accomplishment.

☐ **Cut back tired perennials** – Plants like hostas, peonies and phlox collapse into soggy mush after frost. Grab your secateurs, cut them down to ground level and compost the waste. Leave tougher ones, like sedum and grasses, as they look gorgeous in frost and help feed birds.

☐ **Divide perennials** – Got an overgrown clump (say, daylilies or hardy geraniums)? Dig it up, chop it into chunks with a spade, then replant pieces or give them away.

☐ **Harvest what's left** – Pull up parsnips, snip kale leaves, or collect apples before frost damages them. Don't leave crops rotting – they'll attract pests. If you can't cook straight away, chuck them in a trug for later.

☐ **Wildlife spot prep** – Walk the garden and set up a shelter. Pile of logs or sticks = hedgehog hotel. Bundle of hollow stems or bamboo = bug hotel. Quiet leafy corner left alone = frog/insect heaven.

☐ **Quick greenhouse clean** – Warm soapy water, sponge, quick wipe of glass inside/out. More light means happier seedlings later. Even 20 minutes a week now saves a grim 'deep clean' in February.

🕐 30-MINUTE JOBS

When you have a full half-hour to spare, you can tackle the slightly bigger stuff. Pop on your gloves and get stuck in!

- ☐ **Mulch a border** – Thirty minutes is plenty to cover a bed with compost, leaf mould or bark. Aim for about 5cm thick. Think of it as giving your soil a blanket and a packed lunch to see it through winter.

- ☐ **Lawn care** – Don't panic, no need for golf-green perfection. Give the lawn a final once-over for moss and scatter a bit of autumn lawn feed.

- ☐ **Bulk bulb planting** – Instead of planting bulbs one by one, dig a trench. Line bulbs up, cover, done. In just 30 minutes, you can get through a whole bag of daffs or tulips. It will give you a huge payoff in spring.

- ☐ **Tidy the shed or greenhouse** – Spend 30 minutes stacking pots, sweeping the floor, or sharpening secateurs. Feels boring in autumn, feels glorious in March when everything's ready to go.

- ☐ **Turn the compost heap** – Stick a fork in and mix it around. Add greens (veg peelings, grass) and browns (cardboard, sticks, dried leaves). This helps it rot evenly, so next year you've got rich compost for free.

My Final Thoughts on Autumn Gardening

Autumn gardening is about gently tucking your space in, protecting what you've got and setting up future you for an easier spring. Think of it like laying out your clothes the night before, a small prep job that makes tomorrow infinitely smoother.

For me, 'putting the garden to bed' is almost a ritual. I go round the garden one corner at a time, asking: *What needs protecting? What needs tidying? What can I leave for wildlife?* It's a balance. You're clearing and cutting back, but you're also deliberately leaving a bit of mess, because that's often where the magic (and the hedgehogs) happen.

Do enough to set yourself up for next year, but don't stress about 'finishing'. Nature doesn't do tidy edges; it works in cycles. Leave space for wildlife, accept that not every bulb will bloom and remember you're not just tending plants, you're tending to yourself.

> Take photographs of your autumn garden to document the process of the year. It's so useful to look back on them when you're doing your winter planning, to see what you liked or what you could improve on for next year.

For me, autumn is the season that reminds me why I garden. It's hopeful, grounding and a little bit magical. Every bulb tucked into cold soil, every log pile for a hedgehog, every leaf cleared, it's all a promise that spring will come back.

So, kettle on, jumper zipped, rake in hand. Do a job, big or small.

7
WINTER
Low-Effort Gardening and Planning for Next Year

Winter. The season most gardeners pack away their gloves, close the shed door and decide to 'deal with it in spring'. And I get it... dark mornings, frosty evenings, frozen ground, it doesn't exactly scream 'let's go play in the mud'. But here's the thing, winter isn't just a pause button in the gardening year. It's the hidden season, the quiet stretch where you can do small, simple jobs that pay off massively later on.

For me, winter has always been about balance. Although calm, autumn is fairly busy: you're planting bulbs, raking leaves, cutting things back and trying to get the garden tucked up before the first frost. But winter? It's where you step back, slow down and think ahead. It's less about action and more about steady preparation. And trust me, even when it's freezing, there's still plenty you can do.

The beauty of winter gardening is that it's low effort. You're not going to be out there weeding for hours or planting entire borders in icy rain (unless you're particularly keen, or slightly mad). Instead, winter is about quick wins and smart planning. Protecting plants that need a bit of help, clearing paths and digging in compost or manure so the soil's ready for spring. Even a few minutes outside here and there makes a huge difference.

I think winter gardening is underrated for your mental health. As a firefighter, my shifts can be physically exhausting and mentally draining. Winter can feel heavy in itself: short days, grey skies, everyone a bit more tired and snappy. But there's something about watching your breath in the cold air while topping up the bird feeders or cracking the ice on the bird bath that feels oddly satisfying. Remember, the garden doesn't need you to be full of energy or sunshine, it just needs you to show up.

Another reason winter matters is because it's the season of structure. When all the flowers and leaves have gone, you really see the bones of your garden, the lines of hedges, the curves of borders, the shapes of trees. This is the time to notice what's working, what's not and where you might want to make changes. It's planning season. Take out the notebook, go back to the sketches we did at the beginning and start thinking about next year.

So no, winter isn't a time to abandon your garden. It's a chance to take the pressure off, keep things ticking over and sneak in some small but powerful jobs. By the time spring rolls around, you'll be miles ahead of the game and feeling smug while your neighbour is still battling last year's mess.

So put on a hat, grab a hot drink and let's dive into how to make winter gardening simple, rewarding and – dare I say it – actually enjoyable.

Protecting Tender Plants

One of the biggest winter jobs – and honestly one of the most important, if you don't want heartbreak come spring – is protecting your tender plants. 'Tender' just means plants that don't like the cold. Some will sulk if it gets a bit frosty, others will outright die if left unprotected. Think of them like that mate who insists on wearing shorts all year round (a bit like me). They might make it through, but it's going to be a tough ride.

Protecting tender plants doesn't need to be complicated, expensive or time-consuming. A few simple steps now can mean you get to enjoy those same plants year after year.

Step 1: Know What's Tender
If you're new to gardening, it can be tricky to know which plants need wrapping up. A rough rule of thumb: if the label or garden centre said 'half-hardy' or 'tender perennial', it probably needs a bit of TLC in winter.

Common examples in UK gardens:
- **Dahlias** – the tubers rot if left in frozen ground.
- **Cannas and calla lilies** – gorgeous tropical looks, but not fans of frost.
- **Pelargoniums (geraniums)** – great in pots through summer, but tender in winter.

- **Tree ferns** – love shade and moisture but not freezing winds.
- **Cordylines and palms** – hardy to a point but still benefit from wrapping in very cold areas.

When in doubt: if it looks exotic, chances are it'll want some protection. You can double check your plants online if you'd like to be cautious.

Step 2: Decide: Lift, Wrap or Shelter
You've got three options when it comes to protecting tender plants:

1. **Lift them out**
   – For things like **dahlias** and **gladioli**, dig up the tubers or corms (a type of bulb) once the foliage dies back. Shake off the soil, dry them out for a few days, then store in a box filled with dry compost, sand or sawdust. Keep them somewhere cool, dark and frost-free, like a shed, garage or under the stairs. Don't forget to label them.

2. **Wrap them up**
   – For plants too big to move (like tree ferns, cordylines or cannas in the ground), you can wrap them in **horticultural fleece**. It's a giant plant blanket – cheap, breathable and keeps frost off.
   – Wrap loosely so air can circulate (you don't want plants sweating underneath), and tie with string to stop it blowing away.
   – Cover the top of plants (like tree ferns) with dry straw, bracken or even screwed-up newspaper before wrapping to protect the growing point.

3. **Move them to shelter**
   – Pots are the easiest, just pick them up and move them into a frost-free space like a greenhouse, porch, conservatory, or even a bright windowsill indoors.
   – If pots are too heavy to move, group them against a house wall (south-facing if possible), raise them on pot feet or bricks so they don't sit in soggy soil, and wrap the pot itself in bubble wrap or hessian. The roots are the most vulnerable bit.

Step 3: Keep an Eye Out

Protecting tender plants isn't a 'do it once and forget it' job. Check them every couple of weeks:

- **Stored tubers** – make sure they're not rotting or shrivelling. If too dry, mist lightly; if too damp, let them air.
- **Wrapped plants** – check fleece is still secure after windy weather.

WHY IT MATTERS

Losing plants in winter can be gutting. I'll never forget my first attempt at cannas. I left them outside, thought 'they'll be fine', and come spring they were just mush. Lesson learned. Once you've spent a summer nurturing a plant, it makes sense to spend a few minutes making sure it survives the winter.

And honestly, there's something comforting about tucking plants in for the cold season. Wrapping a tree fern in its fleece scarf, boxing up dahlias like little treasures, then when they bounce back in spring, it's like seeing them wake up after a long sleep.

Keeping the Garden Safe

Winter gardens can be beautiful, but they can also be surprisingly hazardous if you don't give them a bit of care.

Step 1: Tackle the Leaves

Leaves are the main culprit of problems in autumn and early winter. They collect on every surface – paths, patios, decking – and they stay damp. That dampness invites moss and algae, which then make things dangerously slick.

Tips for leaf clearing:
- **Tools:** A broom or stiff brush is usually enough. A leaf blower works too if you've got one, but honestly, a broom does the trick for most small gardens.
- **Little and often:** Do a quick sweep once or twice a week rather than letting piles build up. Five minutes here and there saves you an hour later.
- **Recycling leaves:** Like we touched on for your Autumn jobs, don't bin them! Pile them in a corner to make leaf mould (brilliant mulch in a year or so) or add them to your compost heap.

Step 2: Moss and Algae Control

Moss and algae love the damp, shady corners of winter gardens. Left unchecked, they turn paving into a skating rink.

How to deal with moss/algae:
- **Brush first:** A stiff-bristled broom or wire brush gets rid of loose growth.
- **Hot water:** Pouring a kettle of hot water and scrubbing can kill off small patches without chemicals.
- **Special cleaners:** If it's really bad, you can buy path and patio cleaners from garden centres. Look for pet-safe ones if you've got furry friends around.

Personally, I keep a stiff broom by the back door. After a wet week, I'll give the patio a quick scrub before it builds up. It's one of those low-effort jobs that makes a big difference.

Step 3: Clear Snow and Ice

Now, snow isn't always a regular UK visitor, but when it does show up, it can cause chaos. The key is to keep paths and driveways clear before they turn icy.

- **Shovel snow:** If it's a heavy fall, get it shifted before it compacts into ice.
- **Grit or salt:** Sprinkle grit, sand or table salt to help with traction and melting. (Don't go mad with salt near plants as it can damage soil.)
- **Alternative trick:** Cat litter (the non-clumping kind) works in a pinch for grip on icy steps.

Step 4: Look After Decking

Decking can be the worst offender for accidents in winter; it looks innocent but turns into a skating rink when wet.

- Sweep off leaves as soon as possible.
- Give it a scrub with warm soapy water and a stiff brush occasionally.
- If it's untreated wood, consider an anti-slip treatment or oil in spring to make life easier next winter.

Step 5: Check Lighting

With shorter days, chances are you'll be walking around the garden in the dark more often. A bit of outdoor lighting (solar, mains, or even outdoor battery-powered fairy lights) make paths safer and more welcoming.

I've got a couple of solar lights along my patio, and even in winter they give enough glow to stop me tripping over the cat on the way to the compost bin.

WHY IT'S WORTH DOING

Clearing surfaces might not feel like 'proper gardening', but it's the backbone of winter maintenance. A garden that's safe to walk around is a garden you'll actually use. If the paths are too slippery, you'll avoid going out there altogether, and then all those small winter jobs (like topping up bird feeders or checking fleece on plants) won't get done.

WINTER

Digging in Manure and Improving the Soil

Now, here's a winter job that might not sound glamorous but pays off in spades (literally). Improving your soil in winter is like training in the off-season – it sets you up for big wins when spring and summer arrive. And the simplest, most old-school way to do it? Manure.

Don't panic, you don't need a farmyard or a passing horse and cart to do this. Bagged, well-rotted manure is easy to buy at garden centres, and there are plenty of other options if the idea of manure makes you squeamish. Compost, leaf mould or soil improvers all work, too. But manure has been the gardener's secret weapon for centuries, and once you understand how it works, you'll see why.

WHY BOTHER WITH MANURE?

Plants can only grow as well as the soil allows. If the soil is tired, thin or lacking in nutrients, plants will struggle no matter how much love you give them. Manure (and other organic matter) does three brilliant things:

1. **Adds nutrients** – Manure is full of nitrogen, phosphorus and potassium, the holy trinity of plant food.
2. **Improves structure** – Clay soils become lighter and easier to work; sandy soils hold water better.
3. **Boosts life in the soil** – Worms, fungi and microbes thrive when you add organic matter, and they, in turn, help your plants.

Think of it like feeding the soil, not just the plants. Healthy soil = happy plants.

WELL-ROTTED VS FRESH

This is where a lot of new gardeners panic. 'Do I just grab some fresh manure from a stable and throw it on my plants?' Short answer: **No.** (And if it's not your stable, that's weird.)
- **Fresh manure** is too strong. It can burn plants, stink to high heaven and introduce weeds.

- **Well-rotted manure** (at least 6–12 months old) is crumbly, darker and smells earthy rather than like, well, a farmyard. That's the good stuff.

If you're buying bagged manure, it's already rotted and ready to go. If a local farm or stables offers you some, ask how long it's been sitting. If in doubt, pile it up in a corner of your garden and let it rot for a year before using.

HOW TO DIG IN MANURE

1. **Pick your patch** – Veg beds, borders, anywhere you want healthier soil.
2. **Clear the area** – Pull out any weeds or dead plants first.
3. **Spread the manure** – Scatter it over the soil surface, about 5–10cm thick.
4. **Dig it in** – Use a spade or fork to turn it into the top 15–20cm of soil. Think of it like folding flour into cake batter – it doesn't need to be perfect, just mixed through.
5. **Leave it be** – Winter rain and worms will finish the job for you.

You don't actually have to dig if you don't want to. The 'no-dig' method is popular now – just lay the manure on top like a blanket and let nature work it down. Less work, same benefits.

ALTERNATIVES TO MANURE

If the word manure alone makes your nose wrinkle, don't worry – you've got options:

- **Garden compost** – Made from kitchen scraps and garden waste. Brilliant for borders and veg beds.
- **Leaf mould** – Collected autumn leaves left to rot for a year or two. Fantastic for improving soil texture.
- **Soil improvers** – Shop-bought bags labelled as 'soil improver' often contain a mix of compost and other organic matter. Easy to use.

There's nothing like digging in manure on a crisp winter's day to make you feel like a 'proper' gardener. Yes, your boots will stink and your gloves will need a wash, but come spring, when the soil is rich, dark and full of life, you'll know it was worth it.

Winter Pruning

If there's one gardening job that strikes fear into beginners, it's pruning. The idea of cutting into a plant that's been happily growing all year can feel a bit like playing surgeon without training. 'What if I kill it? What if I cut off the wrong bit? What if it never grows again?'

Plants are tougher than you think. Most of the time, they'll forgive a dodgy cut. And winter is actually the best time to have a go because a lot of plants are dormant.

So, let's go through the big ones: **apple** and **pear trees**, **wisteria** and **reshaping acer trees**. These are the classic winter pruning jobs, and once you've had a go, you'll see it's not as complicated as it sounds.

Tools you'll need:
- Sharp, clean secateurs (for smaller stems).
- Loppers (for thicker branches).
- A pruning saw (for anything too chunky for loppers).

APPLE AND PEAR TREES

If you've got a fruit tree, winter is the ideal time to get them into shape. I talked about spring pruning earlier, but apple and pear trees (not cherry or plum – those prefer summer pruning) love a good haircut in the dormant season.

Why Prune?
- Keeps the tree healthy by removing dead or diseased wood.
- Lets in more light and air, which means better fruit.
- Stops it turning into an unmanageable jungle.

When to Winter Prune?
Any time between November and February, as long as it's not freezing.

How to Prune
1. **Stand back first** – Look at the tree's overall shape. The goal is to create an 'open' shape of branches spreading out with a clear centre.
2. **Remove the 'Three Ds'** – Dead, damaged, diseased. Always start here.
3. **Get rid of crossing branches** – If two branches are rubbing, pick the weaker one and cut it out.

4. **Thin it out** – If it looks crowded, take out some smaller shoots to let light in.
5. **Cut above a bud** – Always prune just above an outward-facing bud (the little bump where new growth comes). That way, new shoots grow outwards, not inwards.

Don't take off more than about 20–25% of the tree in one go. It's better to prune little and often than go wild with the secateurs.

In my own patch, the apple tree gets its yearly trim in January. It's a ritual: a cold morning, a cup of tea steaming beside me, and me talking to the tree as if it can hear ('Don't worry mate, this'll make you stronger').

WISTERIA

Ah, wisteria. The show-off climber that everyone dreams of having. If you've got one, winter is prime pruning time (alongside its summer trim).

Why Prune?
Because left alone, wisteria will take over your entire house. It's a vigorous plant, and pruning keeps it in check while encouraging those famous purple or white flowers.

When to Prune?
January–February.

How to Prune
1. In summer, wisteria sends out long whippy shoots; by winter they will have hardened, but are still obvious. They are long, thin and greener than the rest of the plant, as they are younger, and they often stick out at angles from the main plant.
2. In winter, go back to those shoots and cut them down to 2–3 buds from the main branch to encourage flower buds rather than leafy growth.
3. Cut out any dead, weak or crossing stems.
4. Remove shoots growing into gutters or roof tiles.

My wisteria over the shed is fairly young, I'm really hoping for flowers soon! This gets its haircut in February. Every time, I swear it looks annoyed at me, but fingers crossed by May, it'll reward me with those cascading flowers.

WINTER

SHAPING AN ACER TREE

Why Prune?
To stop the tree getting too dense and remove dead, damaged or crossing branches.

When to Prune?
January–February.

How to Prune
1. Always remove dead, diseased or damaged wood with your first cuts.
2. Remove any crossing or rubbing branches.
3. To shape, think of the overall shape you are aiming for and make small cuts to thin any crowded areas. Acers don't like heavy pruning, so take your time and keep it to a trim.
4. Remember to step back as you go, to make sure you're getting the shape you're aiming for. Think of it as removing clutter and the tree will thank you for it in spring.

OTHER WINTER PRUNING JOBS

- **Deciduous hedges** (like beech or hawthorn): Tidy them up while dormant.
- **Shrubs like dogwood or willow** (grown for colourful stems): Chop them right down to the base in late winter for bold new growth in spring.
- **Grapevines:** These must be pruned in December or January, before sap rises, otherwise they'll 'bleed' badly. This means the sap will flow out of the cut and this can weaken the plant.

A little note: Some people prefer to prune their roses in winter, I tend to prune in spring. Take a look back at the spring pruning guidance for roses (on page 54) if you need a quick reminder.

Pruning isn't about perfection, it's about keeping plants healthy, productive and manageable. If in doubt, cut less rather than more. And remember, plants are far tougher than we give them credit for.

Planting Bare-Root Trees, Hedges and Roses

One of the absolute gems of winter gardening is bare-root planting. If you've never heard of it, don't worry, you're not alone. A lot of beginners head straight for garden centres in spring and summer, loading up with pots of plants. But here's a little secret: winter is when the savvy gardeners get their bargains and their strongest plants.

WHAT DOES 'BARE-ROOT' MEAN?

It's exactly what it sounds like – plants sold without soil around their roots. Instead of being in a pot of compost, they're lifted straight from the ground while dormant (asleep for winter), shaken off and sold as they are. The roots are wrapped in paper, plastic or straw to keep them moist.

Why's this good?
- **Cheaper** – You can buy bare-root trees, roses and hedging plants for a fraction of the price of potted versions.
- **Stronger roots** – Because they grow straight into your soil rather than being pot-bound, they establish faster.
- **Easier to plant** – They're lighter to carry and quicker to get in the ground.
- **More environmentally friendly** – Less plastic, less compost, less faff.

WHAT CAN YOU PLANT BARE-ROOT?

Winter (roughly November to March, when plants are dormant) is bare-root season.

Some classics include:
- **Fruit trees** – Apples, pears, plums and cherries can all be planted as bare roots.
- **Ornamental trees** – From birch to rowan, all sorts are available.
- **Hedges** – Hawthorn, beech, hornbeam, yew, privet – bare-root is by far the most cost-effective way to plant a hedge.
- **Roses** – Many of the best rose nurseries sell bare-root roses in winter; they're cheaper and settle in beautifully.

HOW TO PLANT BARE-ROOT

This is where most people panic ('But it's just roots in a bag!'). Don't worry. Planting bare-root is one of the simplest gardening jobs you'll ever do.

1. **Unpack straight away**
   – Don't leave bare-root plants sitting around for weeks. When they arrive, unwrap them and check the roots are moist. If the roots are not moist, you'll need to give them a soak first.
   – If you can't plant immediately, 'heel them in'. This just means give them a temporary home until you're ready to plant them in their final spot. Dig a shallow trench in the soil, lay the roots in and cover with loose soil. They'll happily wait there a few weeks.

2. **Soak the roots**
   – If you're ready to plant them, give the roots a good soak in a bucket of water for about an hour. This wakes them up and rehydrates them.

3. **Dig a hole (or trench)**
   – For single trees or roses: make a hole wide enough for the roots to spread out comfortably and not be scrunched up.
   – For hedges: dig a trench long enough for your plants, wide enough to spread their roots without bending.

4. **Backfill with soil**
   – Spread the roots out, then backfill gently with soil. Firm it down with your heel to get rid of air pockets, but don't stamp so hard you compact it.

5. **Water in well**
   – Even though it's winter and damp, always give new plants a drink. It helps settle the soil around the roots.

6. **Add support if needed**
   – Trees may need a stake to stop them rocking in the wind while their roots establish. Tie them loosely with a soft tie. There's more info on this in the Spring chapter (see page 57), if you need some guidance.

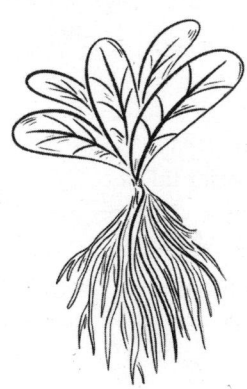

SPACING TIPS FOR BEGINNERS

- **Hedges** – For a dense hedge, plant about 30–40cm apart. If you want a super-thick hedge, you can plant two staggered rows in a zig-zag.
- **Fruit trees** – Dwarf rootstocks can go 3–4m apart; larger ones need more like 4–6m. (Check the label when you buy.)
- **Roses** – Space shrub roses about 60–90cm apart. Climbers can be trained onto supports with more room, ideally around 2m between them so they have space to spread.

WHY WINTER IS BEST

Planting bare-root in winter might feel odd (digging in the cold, when the plant looks like a stick), but it's ideal. Because the plant is dormant, it won't go into shock. Instead, it quietly grows new roots underground all winter. By spring, it's settled and ready to shoot away with strong growth.

Don't be put off by how unimpressive bare-root plants look. They may not come in fancy pots, but they're some of the strongest, cheapest and most rewarding plants you'll ever grow.

Wildlife in Winter

Your garden isn't just about plants and lawns. It's a mini-ecosystem – home to birds, insects, hedgehogs, frogs and a whole range of little visitors. In winter, when food is scarce and the cold bites, these creatures need a helping hand. The good news? With just a few simple steps, you can turn your garden into a winter sanctuary.

We touched on this in the Autumn chapter, but wildlife isn't just 'nice to have' in the garden, it's vital. Birds keep pests in check by eating caterpillars and aphids. Hedgehogs munch through slugs and beetles. Pollinators might be less active in winter, but plenty still shelter in your garden, ready to emerge in spring. By giving them a safe space now, you're helping your garden stay balanced year-round.

And honestly, there's something heartwarming about looking out of your kitchen window on a frosty morning and seeing a robin bobbing about, or a blackbird tugging worms from the soil. It's proof that your garden is alive, even in the quiet season.

BIRDS: KEEPING THEM FED AND WATERED

Birds rely on us heavily in winter, especially when natural food sources like berries and insects are running low. A few small actions make a huge difference:

- **Feeders:** Keep them topped up with seeds, peanuts or fat balls. High-energy foods are essential when it's freezing.
- **Clean regularly:** Dirty feeders spread disease, so give them a scrub with hot, soapy water every couple of weeks. Rinse well before refilling.
- **Bird baths:** Birds need fresh water for drinking and bathing, even in winter. On frosty mornings, crack the ice or add a small ball (like a ping-pong ball) to keep water moving and stop it freezing solid.
- **Variety of food:** Different birds like different things. Nyjer seeds attract finches; mealworms bring in robins. Mix it up for a garden full of colour and song.

I've got a feeder right by my shed, and it's genuinely one of my favourite winter sights, blue tits squabbling over peanuts while I potter about. I also spot Steven the naughty squirrel stealing the birds' food. It makes the cold feel a bit less bleak.

HEDGEHOGS: HELPING THEM HIBERNATE

Hedgehogs are one of the gardener's best friends, and I honestly love them. In winter, they hibernate, but they need somewhere safe to do it. If you didn't get round to it in autumn, now is a great time to give them a helping hand.

- **Log piles or hedgehog house:** Stack logs, twigs and leaves in a quiet corner or buy a ready-made house. Hedgehogs will crawl in and bed down and this will protect them from predators.
- **Avoid strimmers and bonfires:** Always check piles of leaves or sticks before lighting or cutting. Hedgehogs love them, and you don't want any nasty accidents.
- **Extra food:** Before hibernation, hedgehogs bulk up. Leave out cat food (not fish-based) or specialist hedgehog food, plus a shallow dish of water. Never milk, it makes them ill.

FROGS, TOADS AND OTHER VISITORS

If you've got a pond, it's a winter haven. Here's how to keep it safe:

- **Stop it freezing solid:** Place a ball or a stick on the surface. If ice forms, remove the object and you'll keep a small hole open for oxygen exchange.
- **Leaf nets:** These stop your pond filling with soggy leaves, which rot down and upset the balance.
- **Quiet edges:** Frogs and toads may tuck themselves into muddy banks or piles of leaves nearby. Leave them be.

WHY IT'S GOOD FOR YOU TOO

Looking after wildlife isn't just about helping them, it helps us too. Feeding birds gives you daily entertainment. Knowing a hedgehog is tucked into your log pile makes you smile. And every time you leave a little wild space, you're also saving yourself some work.

Wildlife doesn't need fancy setups, just food, water, shelter and a little thought. Do that, and your garden will stay buzzing, chirping and alive, even in the depths of winter.

Fun Winter Garden Projects

Winter might look like a dead season, but it's actually the perfect time for little projects that don't require sweating in the sun or endless weeding. These are the jobs that feel more like play than work, the ones where you get to be a bit crafty, a bit organised and a bit smug because you're quietly setting yourself up for next year while everyone else is hibernating on the sofa.

Here are some of my favourites that anyone can do:

DIY PLANTERS FROM RECYCLED MATERIALS

Winter is prime time to get creative with planters. You're not planting much outside anyway, so why not prepare some quirky containers for spring?

- **Ideas:** Old boots, tin cans, colanders, even broken wheelbarrows. Drill drainage holes, add compost, and you're ready for planting when the weather warms.
- **Why now?** Because come spring you'll be too busy sowing and weeding. Plus, it's a great way to upcycle instead of binning stuff.

PLAN YOUR PLANTING SCHEME

Winter is thinking season. The garden's bare bones are visible, so you can see clearly where gaps are, where you need more colour, or where a new bed might fit.
- **How to do it:** Grab a notebook or go back to your garden map on page 47. Have you been happy with how things have grown? Do you want to add in any new features? Have any new structures altered the sunny spots in the garden? Look at the pictures you took in each season – what worked, what didn't, what might you want more of? This will help you do your sketch for next year.
- **Seed catalogues:** This is where the fun really begins. Curl up with a catalogue or browse online, circling everything you want (and then realistically halving it, because we all get carried away).

I love this stage, it's all about dreams. Every scribble on paper is a promise of what's to come. And the beauty of winter projects is that they don't feel like chores. They're small, creative and rewarding. Each one gives you a sense of progress while the garden itself is resting.

Quick Winter Jobs

The great thing about winter gardening is that you don't need to spend hours outside to make a difference. Short, sharp jobs keep your garden ticking over without freezing your toes off. Whether you've got 10 minutes, 20 minutes, or 30 minutes to spare, there's always something useful (and satisfying) you can do.

 10-MINUTE JOBS

Got a few minutes and a bit of motivation, perfect! Here are some quick jobs that will make you feel productive.

- ☐ **Crack the ice on the bird bath** – Birds need fresh water more than ever in winter, but ice often locks it away. Just nip outside, break the ice and top up with fresh water.

- ☐ **Brush snow or wet leaves off plants** – Snow can weigh down branches and snap them. A quick brush with a broom saves damage. The same goes for soggy leaves sitting in the crown of plants – just flick them off.

- ☐ **Clear the path** – A quick sweep of leaves, ice or mud from your garden path makes it safe to walk on. Nobody wants to end up on their bum when they're carrying the recycling bin.

- ☐ **Check greenhouse ventilation** – Even in winter, greenhouses can get damp and mouldy. Pop in, open the vents for a few minutes and wipe away condensation. Takes no time at all, but keeps plants healthier.

- ☐ **Sow microgreens indoors** – If you're desperate for greenery, grab a tray and some compost, and sprinkle with salad seeds (like rocket or radish). Place on a windowsill. It takes ten minutes and you'll be cutting fresh leaves in a fortnight.

20-MINUTE JOBS

If you have a bit more time, get stuck in with these. A few 20-minute sessions a week and your garden will quietly transform.

- ☐ **Prune wisteria** — In winter, cut back wisteria side shoots to 2–3 buds from the main stem. Don't panic, it's easier than it sounds. You're basically tidying up the long, whippy growths, so the plant's energy goes into the flowers next spring. Go back to page 120 for more info, if needed.

- ☐ **Give tools a quick clean** – Grab a bucket of soapy water, dunk your trowel, secateurs or fork, scrub and then dry them. Even a 20-minute blitz makes a huge difference to how long they last.

- ☐ **Plant bare-root trees or roses** – Bare-root plants arrive in winter when they're dormant. Dig a hole wide enough for the roots, pop the plant in, fill in with soil and firm down with your boot. Water in, if it's not frozen.

- ☐ **Tidy the shed** – Stack pots, coil hoses and chuck out broken bits you'll 'definitely use one day' (spoiler: you won't). It clears space for spring chaos.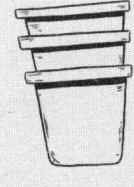

- ☐ **Feed the birds** – Top up feeders with seeds, fat balls or peanuts. It's not just kindness, it's pest control for later, because birds will repay you by eating aphids and caterpillars come spring.

 30-MINUTE JOBS

Half an hour doesn't sound like much, but it's plenty of time to make a visible difference. Have a go at these and then stand back and admire your work!

The beauty of these quick jobs is that none of them are overwhelming. Do a couple here and there, and you'll keep your garden ticking over all winter without ever feeling like you're stuck in a slog.

- ☐ **Dig in compost or manure** – Pick a bed, spread a barrow-load of compost or manure and lightly fork it in. You don't need to dig deep, worms will do the heavy lifting.

- ☐ **Prune apple and pear trees** – Aim for an open 'wine glass' shape, so sunlight and air can get in. Cut out dead or crossing branches first, then shorten some of the longer shoots. Take your time, you don't have to do the whole tree in one go.

- ☐ **Wash pots and seed trays** – Fill a bucket with hot, soapy water and scrub. It feels boring, but clean pots = fewer pests and diseases. Plus, it's oddly satisfying when you stack them all neatly after.

- ☐ **Refresh a compost heap** – Turn the contents with a fork, mix in some browns (cardboard, straw) if it's slimy, and add greens (veg peelings, coffee grounds) if it's too dry.

- ☐ **Plant a hedge** – If you've got bare-root hedge plants, this is the time to get them in. Dig a trench, space plants about 30–40cm apart, drop them in, then backfill with soil. Planting in winter gives them months to settle before summer heat arrives.

My Final Thoughts on Winter Gardening

Winter gardening isn't about long days with muddy knees and aching backs. It's about keeping your garden ticking over with light touches, clever preparation and a bit of dreaming for what's to come.

The beauty of winter gardening is that none of this has to be hard. Even the smallest effort pays back big time. One bag of bulbs tucked into the ground now means a spring display that makes your heart skip. Cracking the ice on a bird bath means sparrows, blackbirds and robins singing for you when everything else feels grey. Spending 20 minutes mulching a border gives you months of healthier plants with less work later.

And beyond the plants, there's you. Don't underestimate the power of stepping outside in winter. The light, the air, the rhythm of small jobs, it all adds up. For me, after a night shift at the fire station, ten minutes topping up the bird feeders or tidying a border does more for my head than hours of staring at a screen ever could.

My advice? Don't shut the door on your garden until spring. Wrap up warm, keep it simple and do a little here and there. Treat it as time for yourself as much as time for your plants.

Get the kettle boiled, get your hat and gloves on, and enjoy your breath clouding in the cold air as you tick off the jobs.

3

STEPPING UP YOUR GARDENING SKILLS

8
ESSENTIAL LAWN CARE TIPS

For some people, a lawn is just that flat bit of green between the house and the shed. For me, it's an obsession. There's something about a freshly cut lawn, stripes shimmering in the sun, the smell of grass clippings in the air. It feels like the heartbeat of my garden.

My obsession started young. One of my chores as a kid was mowing the lawn and I noticed something. In half an hour, the whole garden transformed. Scruffy, messy chaos became neat, calm and ordered. Those stripes gave the space structure and they gave me a sense of satisfaction.

Fast-forward to now, and people know me as 'the lawn guy'. And honestly, I don't mind that one bit. Lawns and the garden have become my therapy. After a stressful shift at the fire station, mowing calms my mind like nothing else. You can't worry about life when you're concentrating on keeping lines straight. Artificial lawns have their place, but for me nothing beats the satisfaction of nurturing real grass and watching it thrive under my care.

But here's the part I really want you to hear: lawn care doesn't have to be complicated. You don't need a degree in horticulture, or a ride-on mower the size of a tractor (no matter how cool that is). You just need to understand the basics and do them consistently. Even if your grass currently looks like a tired doormat, it can bounce back. Lawns are tougher than most people think.

This chapter is here to show you how. From feeding and mowing to fixing bald patches and dealing with dog wee spots, I'll walk you through it. And I promise to keep it simple, beginner-friendly and maybe even a bit fun (yes, fun, this is me we're talking about).

Whether you're starting from scratch or looking to breathe new life into an existing lawn, this chapter has you covered. From soil to seed to maintenance, we'll tackle small jobs, and the bigger ones that will make a real difference to your lawn. We'll also look at common problems and how to fix them. By the end, you won't just know how to look after your lawn, you'll actually want to.

First, let's cover the basics...

The Basics: How to Get Lush, Green Grass

Everyone wants that soft, green carpet you can walk on barefoot. The good news is that it's easier than you think. Forget overcomplicated advice and Instagram-perfect lawns. A healthy lawn boils down to a few simple habits. Get these right and you're 90% there. If you're a lawn newbie, these tips will make the most impact with minimum effort (and skill) required.

1. GETTING TO KNOW YOUR SOIL

Your lawn is only ever as good as the soil beneath it. Grass is a shallow-rooted plant, so it depends heavily on the top layer of soil for food, water and stability.

Here's the quick soil test: grab a handful.

- **Clay soil** feels heavy and sticky, and holds water. Great for nutrients, rubbish for drainage.
- **Sandy soil** will be loose, gritty, and dry quickly. Easy to work, but nutrients wash straight through.
- **Loam** is crumbly, rich and dark. The holy grail.

Don't panic if you don't have loam (I don't either). My garden is clay-heavy, which means it can turn into a bog in winter and crack like concrete in summer. For years, I fought it. Now, I work with it, adding compost in autumn, aerating regularly and overseeding thin patches. The difference is incredible.

Whatever soil you've got, improving it with organic matter (compost, leaf mould or manure) will help your lawn thrive.

ESSENTIAL LAWN CARE TIPS

2. FEED IT (BUT DON'T OVERDO IT)

Grass is greedy, it grows fast, gets chopped back constantly and *still* has to look good. So, yes, it needs food. But here's the golden rule: more fertiliser does not mean better.

For now, just remember to feed lightly, match it to the season and don't overdo it. I'll go into this in more detail later.

3. MOW SMARTER, NOT HARDER

Mowing is the single biggest factor in lawn health. Most people think it's just about keeping grass short, but it's actually about helping the grass grow thicker and stronger.

Here are some general rules:

- **Never cut off more than one-third at once**. If your grass is 9cm, don't cut lower than 6cm. Cutting too much at once stresses the grass, whereas a small trim encourages growth.
- **Raise blades in summer**. Longer grass shades the soil, keeps moisture in and fights weeds.
- **Keep blades sharp**. A clean cut heals fast and looks much neater. A dull blade can tear the grass and cause brown spots. Once or twice a season is enough to sharpen the blades – always protect your hands and make sure the mower is off at the mains. Use a sharpening stone and follow the angle of the blade edge. If you prefer, you can get this done professionally.

My first big mistake? Scalping the lawn super short to 'save time between mows'. It looked neat for about a day. Then the sun hit, and the whole thing fried. Now I mow higher, more often, and mix up the direction each week to avoid compacting the soil and creating grooves.

Yes, I do use an electric mower with a roller, because I'm stripe-obsessed. The satisfaction of those crisp lines never gets old. But don't worry, you can still get the same crisp results with a well-kept manual mower.

4. WATER WISELY

Here's where I have to acknowledge another minor contradiction. Throughout this book I've been preaching 'little and often'. But with watering lawns, that rule doesn't work. If you just sprinkle a little every day, you're basically teaching your grass to be lazy. It'll keep roots shallow and cry the second the soil dries.

Think of it like kids and snacks: if you give them a biscuit every half hour, they'll never sit down for a proper meal. Lawns are the same. They want a good soak, not a constant dribble.

General rules:
- **Water deeply, less often** (once a week max through spring and summer) – that way, roots grow down searching for moisture. You can water less often as the weather changes, and the grass is dormant in winter so watering is not necessary.
- **Mornings are best** – less evaporation, and less chance of fungal problems. If you are short on time, you could consider putting a sprinkler on a timer to do the job for you.
- **Rainwater beats tap water** – if you can collect it in a butt. You can also skip the weekly watering session if there has been a good downpour (which in the UK is highly likely!) – just make sure the soil is soaked deep down rather than just on the surface.

And don't panic if your lawn goes brown in a drought. Grass naturally goes dormant and bounces back with rain. I've seen mine look like a patch of straw mid-July, then recover beautifully in September.

5. OVERSEED BARE PATCHES

No matter how good you are, every lawn gets bald spots, whether it's from kids, pets, shade, or overenthusiastic fertiliser (yep, guilty again). The fix is overseeding – simply sprinkling fresh grass seed into the gaps. Aim to do this in early autumn or from March to May. Here's a beginner's step-by-step guide:

1. **Rake or fork the area** to loosen the soil.
2. **Scatter seed evenly**. Consider the type of seed you need based on your lawn use. For high-traffic areas you'll need a tougher, quicker-growing seed and for a more ornamental lawn you can go with something a bit softer. There's also 'mixed use' seed, so you can get the best of both.

3. **Rake lightly**, so the seeds come in contact with the soil.
4. **Water gently**, to avoid displacing any seeds.
5. **Protect from birds** or other pests with fleece or twigs.

That's it! Within a couple of weeks, green shoots will pop up. Don't overthink it – it really is that simple.

Healthy lawns aren't complicated. Start with decent soil, feed sensibly, mow smarter, water properly and overseed when needed. Get those basics down, and your grass will thank you with stripes that make the neighbours jealous.

New Lawns: Starting from Scratch

If you're beginning with a bare patch of soil, or something that resembles a builder's yard – don't worry, you're in the perfect place to start fresh.

LAYING TURF

If choosing to lay turf, make sure you follow these easy steps for best results. Timing will be important: aim to lay during either March–May or September–early November, when the soil is moist and not too cold.

1. **Clear the area of weeds**, stones and any old grass. You'll need a clean, even base to start with.
2. **Understand your soil type**, as noted on page 136. If it's clay, add some sand or compost to help drainage. For sandy soil, mix in some organic matter, such as compost or well-rotted manure.
3. **Prepare the soil** by loosening the top 10–15cm, then rake it to smooth it out and level it.
4. **Sprinkle some pre-turf fertiliser** over the area and lightly rake it in to give the turf a good start.
5. **Lay the turf** by starting along a straight edge. Align each roll, but don't overlap. Use a plank to walk across it, to avoid leaving footprints and creating dips.
6. **Trim and tidy** the edges.
7. **Water thoroughly** – you'll need to keep it damp for at least 3 weeks.

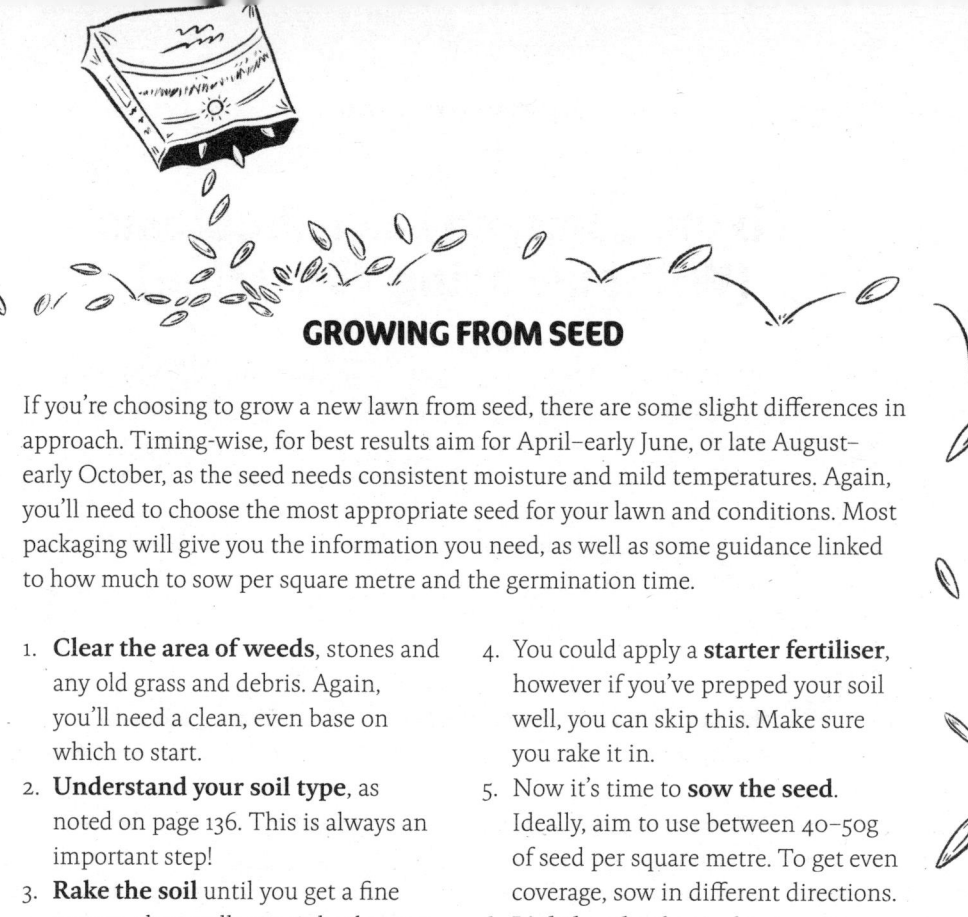

GROWING FROM SEED

If you're choosing to grow a new lawn from seed, there are some slight differences in approach. Timing-wise, for best results aim for April–early June, or late August–early October, as the seed needs consistent moisture and mild temperatures. Again, you'll need to choose the most appropriate seed for your lawn and conditions. Most packaging will give you the information you need, as well as some guidance linked to how much to sow per square metre and the germination time.

1. **Clear the area of weeds**, stones and any old grass and debris. Again, you'll need a clean, even base on which to start.
2. **Understand your soil type**, as noted on page 136. This is always an important step!
3. **Rake the soil** until you get a fine texture, then walk over it heel to toe to firm it. Lightly rake again, to even it out. This step prevents lumps and helps the grass seed establish evenly.
4. You could apply a **starter fertiliser**, however if you've prepped your soil well, you can skip this. Make sure you rake it in.
5. Now it's time to **sow the seed**. Ideally, aim to use between 40–50g of seed per square metre. To get even coverage, sow in different directions.
6. **Lightly rake** the seed in to cover with a thin layer of soil.
7. **Water gently** and aim to keep the soil evenly moist until it germinates. Usually, this will take 1–3 weeks, depending on the temperature.

Fixing Common Lawn Problems (Without Losing Your Mind)

Every lawn has problems. Even the most well-loved lawns can hit bumps along the way (mine included). It doesn't matter how much love you give it, at some point you'll spot a bald patch, a weed, or a mysterious yellow circle staring back at you. Here's the good news: none of it is fatal. Lawns are tougher than they look, and with a bit of know-how you can fix most issues quickly (and without chemicals). In this section we'll explore practical solutions for common issues.

Let's break down the most common culprits:

MOSS

If moss is taking over, it's not really the moss's fault. Moss is a symptom of unhappy grass. It moves in when conditions aren't right.

Why it happens
- Too much shade.
- Poor drainage or compacted soil.
- Scalped grass (cut too short).
- Weak grass from lack of feed.

How to fix it
1. **Rake or scarify it out** – Yes, your lawn will look terrible for a week. Yes, your neighbours will judge. But it's the only way to clear it.
2. **Improve conditions** – Aerate compacted soil, thin out overhead branches to let in more light, or raise your mower blades so the grass isn't stressed.
3. **Feed the lawn** – Healthy grass will naturally outcompete moss.

Don't waste money on chemical moss killers. They blacken the moss, but if you don't fix the underlying problem, it'll be back before you've put the kettle on.

CLOVER

Some people see clover as the enemy. Personally, I don't mind a bit; it stays green in summer and bees love the flowers. But if you want that classic all-grass look, you'll need to manage it.

Why it happens
Clover thrives in poor soil with low fertility. Basically, it's a sign your grass is hungry.

How to fix it
1. **Feed the lawn** – A balanced, organic fertiliser will give grass the upper hand.
2. **Hand-weed small patches** – A lawn weeder (a long-handled tool) pops clover out by the root. Very satisfying.
3. **Overseed thin areas** – Thicker grass leaves less room for clover to spread.

Or... embrace it. A bit of clover isn't the end of the world. Think of it as free pollinator food and a built-in insurance policy against drought.

ANTS

Ants aren't the most destructive pest there is, but their anthills can make a lawn lumpy and awkward to mow.

Why they appear
Ants love dry, sandy soil and sunny spots.

How to fix it
1. **Brush anthills flat** before mowing, so you don't smear soil everywhere.
2. **Improve soil** by adding compost or topdressing. Ants prefer poor, dry ground.
3. **Nematodes** (yes, again) can be used against ants too, although they're less commonly needed.
4. **Live with them** (within reason) – A few ants aren't harmful, and they even aerate the soil. It's only when anthills multiply that it's worth tackling.

LEATHERJACKETS (AKA LAWN VILLAINS IN DISGUISE)

If your grass looks like it's dying from underneath, with random bare patches, leatherjackets might be the culprit. These are the larvae of crane flies (daddy long-legs). They live in the soil and munch on grass roots.

Spot the signs
- Grass lifts up easily like a carpet.
- Birds (especially starlings) peck at the lawn more than usual.
- Patches thin out even when conditions should be fine.

How to fix it
1. **Nematodes** – These are microscopic worms that specifically target leatherjackets. You water them into the soil and let nature do the rest. No chemicals, safe for pets and kids.
2. **Encourage birds** – They're your allies here. More feeders = more natural pest control.
3. **Overseed patches** – Once the grubs are gone, fill in the bare spots with fresh seed.

It can take a season or two to fully recover, but with patience, lawns bounce back.

DOG WEE PATCHES

Even though I don't have a dog myself, this is the number one lawn problem I get asked to fix. People adore their pets, but not the yellow patches they leave behind.

Why it happens

Dog urine is high in nitrogen. In small doses, nitrogen is great (it's what makes grass green). But too much in one spot is like tipping an entire bag of fertiliser in one patch. You can identify it by a patch of burnt grass in the middle, with a suspiciously greener ring around the outside.

How to prevent it

1. **Flush with water** – If you catch your dog in the act, pour a watering can over the spot. It dilutes the urine before it burns the grass.
2. **Create a toilet zone** – Gravel, bark, or even a patch of artificial turf. Train your dog to use it and save the rest of the lawn.
3. **Diet and neutralisers** – Some products (like 'dog rocks' in the water bowl) claim to neutralise urine before it hits the ground. Results vary, but some owners swear by them. Always check with your vet before making changes.
4. **Spread the load** – If your dog goes in the same corner every time, encourage them to move around. That way, no single patch takes the brunt.

How to fix the damage

1. **Rake out** the dead grass.
2. **Loosen the soil** with a fork.
3. **Sprinkle fresh seed** and a bit of compost.
4. **Water regularly** until it fills in.

The key is don't stress. Dog spots are annoying, but completely fixable.

BALD PATCHES

Every lawn gets them. Luckily, they're the easiest fix of all.

How to repair
1. **Rake out** any dead grass.
2. **Loosen the soil** with a fork.
3. **Add a sprinkle of compost** or topsoil.
4. **Overseed** with grass seed.
5. **Water lightly** and keep off until new growth appears.

Top tip: overseed in spring or autumn when conditions are perfect for germination. Summer seedlings are harder to keep alive without daily watering.

THE BIG PICTURE

Here's what I want you to remember: none of the above problems are fatal. Moss, clover, ants, dog wee, bald patches – every single one is fixable with a bit of patience and consistency. The trick is to treat the cause, not just the symptom.

And don't beat yourself up if your lawn isn't 'perfect'. Perfection doesn't exist (unless you're looking at Wembley). Your goal is healthy, usable grass, not a show lawn you're scared to walk on.

A few weeds don't ruin your lawn. A bit of moss won't kill the vibe. The joy of a lawn is living on it. Football, picnics, dogs, kids, or just you with a brew admiring the stripes.

The Big Jobs (Explained Simply)

When people see me out on the lawn with a scarifier or aerator, they sometimes think I've lost the plot. From the outside, it looks like I'm ripping my grass to shreds or punching holes all over it. My neighbours have definitely raised an eyebrow once or twice. But here's the truth, those jobs are the backbone of lawn care. And let's be honest, it's not the weirdest thing I do in my garden.

The funny thing is, none of them are actually complicated. They sound technical – 'scarification', 'aeration', 'topdressing' – but in reality they're just fancy words for jobs you can do with a rake, a fork and a bit of compost. Done once or twice a year, these jobs will transform your lawn from 'meh' to 'wow'.

Let's break them down:

SCARIFICATION – CLEARING OUT THE JUNK

Scarification is basically a deep clean for your lawn. Over time, dead grass, moss and bits of debris build up at the base of the grass. This layer is called 'thatch'. A little bit is fine, but too much chokes your lawn. It's like trying to breathe through a scarf.

How to know if you need it
- Your lawn feels spongy underfoot.
- Water sits on the surface after rain.
- Moss is spreading like wildfire.

How to do it
1. **Choose your tool** – For small or medium-sized lawns, a spring-tine rake is enough (long flexible metal tines, often fan-shaped). For bigger patches, hire or buy a scarifier machine.
2. **Pick the right time** – You want to be doing this in spring (lightly scarify) or autumn (the main event). Never in summer heat or winter cold.
3. **Go for it** – Rake firmly through the grass, pulling up moss and thatch. Don't panic if it looks worse afterwards, patchy and scruffy is normal.
4. **Tidy up** – Collect all the debris for compost.
5. **Repair** – Overseed straight afterwards. Fresh seed fills the gaps and helps the lawn recover quickly.

My first scarification was a shocker. I thought I'd destroyed my lawn; it looked like a bald cat. But within weeks, fresh green growth came through, and I was hooked.

AERATION – LETTING YOUR LAWN BREATHE

Compacted soil is one of the biggest reasons lawns struggle. All that walking, playing and even just rain pressing down squashes the soil so roots can't breathe. Aeration is simply poking holes in the ground so water, air and nutrients can get to the roots.

Signs you need it
- Grass looks thin no matter what you do.
- Water pools after rain.
- The soil feels rock-hard when you try to dig.

How to do it
- **Fork method** – Stick a garden fork into the lawn about 10–15cm deep. Wiggle it back and forth to open the soil a little. Repeat every 10–15cm.
- **Hollow-tine aerator** – Unlike a garden fork, the prongs of this tool are hollow and pull out little plugs of soil. It looks rough, and like there are mini brown sausages scattered all over your garden, but it relieves compaction properly. This is my favourite method.
- **When?** – Spring or autumn, when grass is actively growing, so it can recover.

Top tip: After aerating, brush compost, sand or topdressing mix into the holes. This keeps channels open and improves soil long-term.

OVERSEEDING – FILLING THE GAPS

Overseeding is basically sprinkling new grass seed into your existing lawn to make it thicker, greener and more resistant to weeds. It's best done in autumn.

Why it works
- Bare patches disappear.
- Fresh grasses improve colour and texture.
- Thick lawns naturally outcompete weeds and moss.

How to do it
1. **Prep** – Mow the lawn and rake to expose the soil.
2. **Seed** – Scatter evenly, about 25–30g per square metre. Don't dump a pile in one spot (been there, done that).
3. **Rake in lightly** – Seeds need contact with soil, not to be buried too deep.
4. **Water gently** – Keep the soil damp until seedlings are established (2–3 weeks).
5. **Keep off** – Avoid walking on it until it thickens up.

TOPSOIL, TOPDRESSING AND SAND – WHAT'S THE DIFFERENCE?

This is where people get confused. Let's keep it simple:

- **Topsoil** – Nutrient-rich soil you use for starting a new lawn or for filling large dips. Think of it as a base layer.
- **Topdressing** – A thin mix of soil, sand and organic matter spread over the surface of an existing lawn. Improves drainage, smooths bumps and feeds the grass.
- **Sand** – Not a fertiliser! It's used only in mixes to improve drainage in heavy clay soils. On its own, it can starve your grass.

When to topdress
After scarifying and aeration, spread a thin layer of topdressing and brush it into holes. It keeps the soil healthy and seed protected.

Rule of thumb
Topsoil for building your lawn; topdressing for maintaining; sand only as part of a mix.

PUTTING IT ALL TOGETHER

Here's how I tackle the big jobs in my own garden each year:

Spring – Light scarify, light aerate, overseed bare patches.
Summer – No big jobs here, just watering and mowing.
Autumn – Full scarify, deep aerate, overseed the whole lawn and finish with a topdress.
Winter – Let it rest. No big jobs needed.

It's not rocket science, it's just routine. A few hours a year, a few basic tools, and your lawn will thank you with thick, healthy growth all year long.

Seasonal Lawn Care

One of the secrets to a good lawn is treating it like a year-round project. It's not a full-time job (don't worry!), but a rhythm that follows the seasons. Grass doesn't behave the same way in spring as it does in summer, so neither should you. Think of it like looking after yourself: sometimes you need fuel, sometimes you need rest, sometimes you just need a trim.

Here's how to work with your lawn, season by season:

SPRING – WAKE-UP CALL

Spring is when your lawn shakes off winter and starts growing again. The soil warms, the daylight stretches and suddenly it's alive. The trick is not to barge in too hard, too soon.

What to do:
- **First, mow** – Set your mower high. Don't scalp it, just give it a gentle trim. Lower the blades gradually over the next few weeks.
- **Light scarify/rake** – Clear away moss and winter debris. A spring-tine rake does the job.
- **Aerate (lightly)** – Push a garden fork in every 15–30cm to let in air and improve drainage.
- **Overseed** – Bare patches? Sprinkle seed, rake it in and keep it damp.
- **Feed** – A spring lawn feed (higher in nitrogen) gives a green boost and helps kick-start growth.

My favourite spring moment? The first set of stripes. They make me feel human again after a long winter.

SUMMER – SURVIVAL MODE

This is the season when lawns take the most abuse – kids, pets, parties and heatwaves all gang up on it. Your goal isn't perfection, it's survival.

What to do:
- **Raise the mower blades** – Cut at 5–7cm. Longer grass shades the soil and holds moisture better.
- **Ease off mowing frequency** – Once every 10–14 days is fine in a hot spell.
- **Water wisely** – Lawns cope with a bit of brown. If you water, do it deeply once a week, not a sprinkle every day.
- **Spot repair** – Sprinkle seed on worn spots (by the goalposts or barbecue zone) and water it in.
- **Weeding** – Hand-weed daisies, clover or dandelions before they spread.

Top tip: Don't stress if your lawn goes brown – it's not dead, just dormant. It'll bounce back with rain.

AUTUMN – RESET BUTTON

If you only go 'all in' once a year, make it autumn. The soil's still warm, there's regular rain and grass is growing strong. It's the perfect time to repair summer damage and prepare for winter.

What to do:
- **Scarify properly** – Rake out moss and thatch. Yes, it'll look awful for a couple of weeks. Yes, it's worth it.
- **Deep aeration** – Use a fork or, better still, a hollow-tine aerator at 10–15cm intervals to relieve compaction and improve drainage.
- **Overseed the whole lawn** – Scatter seed to thicken it up. Brush in some compost or topsoil to protect it.
- **Autumn feed** – Use a low-nitrogen, high-potassium feed. It strengthens roots and prepares grass for the cold.
- **Keep mowing** – Growth won't stop until November. Gradually raise the blades for the last cuts before winter.

Honestly, autumn lawn care is my happy place. Scarify, overseed, aerate – it's the holy trinity. By spring, the difference is night and day.

ESSENTIAL LAWN CARE TIPS

WINTER – REST AND RESIST

Winter is downtime. The lawn hunkers down and so should you. Don't over-fuss it. What to do:

- **Stay off frosty grass** – Walking on frozen blades causes them to snap and scar.
- **Clear leaves** – Don't let them sit and smother the grass.
- **Only mow if necessary** – If the grass is still growing and the ground is firm, give it a high cut. Otherwise, leave it alone.
- **Maintenance jobs** – Sharpen mower blades, clean tools and plan for next year.

Think of winter as the lawn's nap. Let it rest, keep it tidy and don't wake it unless you really need to.

Seasonal lawn care is all about rhythm. Do the right things at the right time, and your lawn will bounce back year after year. Miss a job? Don't panic. Grass is resilient. With a bit of mowing, feeding, scarifying and overseeding at the right moments, even the patchiest lawn can turn into something worth showing off.

Feeding Your Lawn

If mowing is the haircut and watering is the shower, then feeding is the roast dinner. Your lawn is hungry. It's constantly being walked on, cut back, played on and expected to stay lush and green. Without food, it just can't keep up.

The tricky part is this: feeding can be one of the best things you do for your lawn, or one of the worst. Too little, and your grass struggles along, thin and pale. Too much, and you scorch it, leaving brown patches that take weeks to recover. I learned that lesson the hard way. One spring, I thought I'd be clever and double the dose of fertiliser. Within days my lawn had yellow stripes like a dodgy football pitch. It grew back eventually, but my family still laugh about my 'crop circle' summer.

THE NPK BASICS

Every lawn feed comes with three numbers on the bag, written as **NPK**. They stand for the three main nutrients grass needs:

> N = Nitrogen, which makes it green and leafy.
> P = Phosphorus, which helps roots grow strong.
> K = Potassium, which builds toughness and resilience.

Different seasons need different balances. Give high nitrogen in spring and you'll get a lush green boost. In autumn, though, you want lower nitrogen and more potassium, so the grass toughens up for winter.

HOW MUCH TO FEED THROUGH THE YEAR

- **Spring:** Your lawn is waking up hungry. A spring feed with more nitrogen gets it going.
- **Summer:** Keep it light. Overfeeding in heat can stress the grass.
- **Autumn:** This is the big one. Use a feed that strengthens roots rather than forcing leafy growth.
- **Winter:** Don't bother. The grass is dormant and won't use it.

Think of it like meals: spring is breakfast, summer is a light lunch, autumn is a hearty dinner – by winter all you need is a nap.

HOW TO FEED WITHOUT WRECKING IT

The main mistakes beginners make are uneven spreading, feeding at the wrong time, or thinking 'more is better'. Stick to these rules instead:

1. **Spread evenly** – Patchy feeding = patchy lawn. Use a spreader if you've got one, or go slowly by hand.
2. **Water it in** – Either apply before rain or give it a light watering yourself.
3. **Follow the dosage** – The instructions on the bag aren't suggestions, they're there to stop you frying your lawn.
4. **Don't feed stressed grass** – If it's already brown from drought, wait for rain to revive it first.

MY ROUTINE

Here's what I do in my own garden:
- Feed once in spring for that fresh green boost.
- Leave it in summer unless the grass looks really tired.
- Feed again in autumn to toughen it up for winter.
- Skip winter altogether.

Simple, effective and no scorch marks.

Feeding your lawn is about consistency, not excess. Stick to the right feed at the right time and resist the temptation to 'double up'. Do that, and your lawn will reward you with steady, healthy growth instead of crispy regret.

Simple Lawn Care Schedule

	Spring	Summer	Autumn	Winter
Mow height	7–10cm (first mow); 4–5cm (thereafter)	4–5cm (raise to 6–7cm, if hot/dry)	4–5cm; raise to 6–7cm for last cut	Only mow if mild and dry, keep at 6–8cm
Scarify	X (light)		X (main)	
Aerate	X		X	
Overseed	X		X	
Feed	X (nitrogen-rich spring feed)		X (potassium-rich autumn feed)	
New turf	X		X	
New seed	X		X	
Weekly water	X (if dry)	X		

My Lawn Care Philosophy

If you've stuck with me this far, you know I *love* my lawn. Stripes, mowing heights, scarifying, overseeding, I could talk about them for hours (and often do). But here's the thing: for me, lawns have never just been about the grass. They've always been about something deeper.

When my mum was poorly, mowing the lawn became my escape. It was the one job that was mine, a slice of order when everything else felt messy and out of control. The hum of the mower, the smell of cut grass, those neat green lines, it gave me peace when I needed it most. Even now, decades later, I feel that same sense of calm every time I finish a mow. The lawn isn't just a patch of grass, it's therapy with stripes.

That's why I'll always argue that lawns are worth the effort. But I'll also be the first to say they don't need to be perfect. Perfection is overrated. A few weeds here and there won't ruin your life. Grass turning brown in a heatwave isn't failure, it's just your lawn having a little nap. What matters is that your lawn works for you. Maybe that means a football pitch for the kids, a picnic spot in summer, or simply a green backdrop for your borders.

I've killed patches with fertiliser, scalped it with the mower, overseeded badly (twice) and spent a whole afternoon chasing birds off newly sown seed. And you know what, the grass still came back. That's the beauty of lawns, they're resilient. Just like us.

These days, my philosophy is simple. Do what you can, when you can, and don't beat yourself up about the rest. A light feed here, a mow there, maybe a scarify or overseed when the season's right. Keep it healthy enough to bounce back, but don't let it take over your weekends.

Because the real joy of a lawn isn't in staring at it, it's in living on it. It's barefoot steps on a summer evening. It's kids running through a sprinkler. It's sitting down after a long day, brew in hand, thinking, *'Yeah, that'll do.'*

And if you take just one thing from this chapter, let it be this: **lawns, like life, don't need to be flawless**. They just need a bit of care, a bit of patience and the willingness to laugh at the mistakes along the way.

9
MULCHING, WEEDING AND KEEPING THINGS TIDY

If we're being honest, mulching, weeding and tidying aren't the parts of gardening that make it onto glossy Instagram reels. No one's rushing out to film themselves hauling a trug of dandelions or spreading compost in the rain. These are the 'behind-the-scenes' jobs, the ones that keep the garden ticking along quietly in the background. And yet, they're the foundation of everything.

Think of it like this: a rock band needs the drummer. They're not flashy, they don't get the solos, but without them the whole thing falls apart. In gardening, mulching and weeding are the drummers. If you ignore them, the rest of the show sounds off.

I'll admit it, for years I thought weeding was the ultimate chore. I'd leave it too long, then spend an entire weekend crawling through borders like a soldier in boot camp, pulling out a jungle that had practically evolved its own ecosystem. By the end, I'd be sweaty, grumpy and vowing never to let it get that bad again. Of course, the weeds didn't care and they were back within weeks. It wasn't until I switched to the 'little and often' approach (five minutes here, ten minutes there) that I realised weeding doesn't have to be painful. In fact, it can even feel therapeutic if you let it.

Mulching was another revelation for me. The first time I spread a layer of compost over the borders, I thought I was just making them look neat. What I didn't realise was that I'd just given the soil a blanket, a meal and a shield against weeds all in one. A few months later, the plants were healthier, I was watering less and my borders looked like they'd been given a glow-up. I was hooked.

And tidying? Well, let's be honest, the garden will never stay tidy for long. But keeping on top of the basics – sweeping paths, clearing leaves, trimming edges – it all makes the whole place feel calmer, more welcoming, more like somewhere you actually want to sit with a brew.

So, while these jobs might not sound glamorous, they're the ones that make the biggest difference. In this chapter, we're going to strip them down to the basics: what mulch actually is, how to tackle weeds without breaking your back, and why sometimes leaving things a little 'messy' is actually the best thing you can do for your garden (and your sanity).

Mulching: The Gardener's Secret Weapon

Let's start with mulching, because once you 'get it', it feels like the ultimate gardening cheat code. Honestly, mulching is one of those things that sounds fancy and complicated (like something that professional gardeners with their Latin plant labels and immaculate borders do). But in reality, it's as simple as giving your soil a protective blanket.

And the best part is, it does about five different jobs for you at once. It improves the soil, keeps weeds down, locks in moisture, protects roots from temperature swings and makes the whole garden look instantly tidier. All from just spreading a layer of stuff on top of the soil.

WHAT ACTUALLY IS MULCH?

At its simplest, mulch is anything you spread on top of your soil. That's it. You're not digging it in (although, over time, it will naturally mix down). You're just covering the surface with a protective layer.

There are two main types:
- **Organic mulches** – Compost, bark chips, leaf mould, well-rotted manure, straw. These not only protect the soil but also break down over time and improve it.
- **Inorganic mulches** – Gravel, slate chippings, landscaping fabric. These don't feed the soil, but they're useful for suppressing weeds and creating a certain look.

For me, organic mulches are the holy grail because they protect the soil now and improve it long-term. It's like getting a duvet and a vitamin pill in one.

WHY MULCHING WORKS (THE BENEFITS)

Here's why I swear by it:

1. **Moisture Retention** – Mulch acts like a lid on your soil. In summer, it stops water evaporating so fast. In winter, it prevents rain from washing nutrients away. Less watering for you, happier roots for your plants.
2. **Weed Control** – Mulch blocks light from reaching weed seeds. No light, no germination. You'll still get the odd dandelion or dock poking through, but trust me, it's nothing compared to leaving the soil bare.
3. **Soil Improvement** – Organic mulches slowly break down, feeding the soil and improving its structure. Clay becomes less sticky, sandy soil holds more moisture and everything just works a little better.
4. **Temperature Regulation** – In summer, mulch keeps roots cool. In winter, it acts as insulation against frost. Think of it as central heating for your plants.
5. **Aesthetic Glow-Up** – This one's underrated. A freshly mulched border instantly looks neat and cared for, even if you've done nothing else. It's the gardening equivalent of a fresh haircut.

THE BEST MULCHES TO USE

So, what should you actually use? Here are my go-tos:
- **Compost** – Homemade or shop-bought, this is my number one. It feeds the soil beautifully and looks neat. Take a look at the section on making your own compost (page 59), if you need to.
- **Leaf mould** – If you've bagged up autumn leaves, a year later you've got gardener's gold. Crumbly, dark and free.
- **Bark chips/wood chips** – Great for paths and around shrubs. They last a while and suppress weeds well.
- **Well-rotted manure** – Brilliant for veg patches and hungry plants like roses. Just make sure it's rotted, as fresh manure will scorch plants.
- **Straw** – Excellent for strawberries (keeps fruit off damp soil) and veg patches.

What I *don't* recommend is using fresh grass clippings as mulch. They're too wet and compact into a slimy mess that blocks air. I tried it once in a fit of 'waste nothing' enthusiasm and ended up with a mat that killed the seedlings underneath. Never again.

WHEN TO MULCH

Timing makes a difference. The golden rule is to mulch when the soil is moist and weed-free, so you're locking in the good stuff, not the problems.

- **Spring (April/May)** – Locks in spring rain and preps beds for summer. Great for flower borders.
- **Autumn (September/October)** – My favourite time. You're feeding the soil for winter, protecting roots from frost, and tucking the garden in.

You can mulch in summer too especially if beds are drying out fast, but water thoroughly first or you'll just trap dryness underneath.

HOW TO MULCH: STEP-BY-STEP

Don't overthink it. Here's my foolproof method:

1. **Clear the area** – Pull out visible weeds, cut back dead growth and tidy the soil surface.
2. **Water if needed** – If the soil is bone dry, give it a good soak first. Mulch locks in moisture but it can't create it.
3. **Spread the mulch** – Aim for about 5cm thick. Too thin and weeds will still push through; too thick and you risk suffocating your plants.
4. **Keep stems clear** – Don't pile mulch right up against plant stems or tree trunks, as it can cause rot. Leave a little 'collar' of bare soil around them.
5. **Top up annually** – Most organic mulches break down over time, which is part of the magic. Just top it up each year to keep the benefits going.

And that's it. No digging, no heavy lifting. Just spread, step back and admire how much smarter your garden looks.

In my garden, autumn mulching has become a ritual. After a busy summer of constant watering, feeding and weeding, autumn is when I finally slow down. I'll spend some time wheelbarrowing compost from my bin to the borders, spreading it with a rake and standing back to admire the 'after' shot. It feels like tucking the garden into bed for winter.

The kids sometimes help too, although 'helping' usually means tipping half the barrow onto the lawn and jumping in it. Still, they love the sense of being involved, and honestly, I don't mind the chaos. By spring, the soil looks fantastic, the plants thank me with lush growth and I've done half the work for myself already.

COMMON MULCHING MISTAKES (AND HOW TO AVOID THEM)

Even though mulching is simple, there are a few rookie errors worth avoiding:
- **Too much mulch** – A thick, soggy blanket can suffocate roots. Stick to a 5cm layer, not a whole duvet.
- **Wrong material** – Fresh woodchips placed directly onto veg beds steal nitrogen as they rot, leaving plants hungry. Use them for paths or ornamentals instead.
- **Forgetting to weed first** – Mulch won't kill established weeds. You'll just be giving them a cosy duvet. Always weed first.
- **Mulching dry soil** – Remember, mulch traps what's there. Water first, then mulch.

WHY MULCHING IS WORTH IT

I often say that mulching is one of the least glamorous jobs with the biggest payoff. It's like servicing your car, boring on the day, but it saves you endless trouble later. Skip it, and you'll be watering more, weeding more and wondering why your soil looks tired. Do it, and your plants thrive with less effort.

And for beginners, it's such a confidence booster. You don't need to know the proper names of anything, you don't need fancy tools, just a bag of compost and a rake. Spread it out, and you'll see the difference within weeks.

When friends ask me what the single best thing they can do for their garden is, nine times out of ten I say, 'Mulch'. It's that simple.

Weeding: The Least Painful Ways to Tackle It

Let's talk about weeds.

The word alone is enough to make most gardeners sigh. They sneak in overnight, grow faster than anything you actually planted, and somehow survive droughts, floods and every bit of neglect you throw at them. Meanwhile, the plants you *want* to grow look like they need constant babysitting.

When I first started gardening, I used to think weeds were proof that I was doing something wrong. Like the garden police were going to show up and tell me I'd failed because I had dandelions in the borders. The truth is every garden has weeds. Even the most pristine show gardens you see in magazines are constantly weeded behind the scenes. Weeds are just part of gardening – a very persistent, sometimes annoying part.

But here's the good news: dealing with them doesn't have to be back-breaking or soul-destroying. You don't need to spend hours on your knees every weekend to keep on top of it. With a few smart habits, the right tools and a little acceptance that 'perfectly weed-free' isn't realistic, you can stay ahead without losing your mind.

WHAT EVEN IS A WEED?

This is one of those gardening questions that sounds simple but gets philosophical fast. The basic definition is: **a weed is any plant growing where you don't want it.**

That means a dandelion in your lawn is a weed. But if you've got a wildflower patch and you *like* the dandelions, suddenly they're not weeds anymore. Some people even eat dandelion leaves in salads. The same with nettles. Painful in the wrong place, brilliant for butterflies in the right one.

So before you start yanking things out, it's worth asking yourself, is this plant actually causing a problem, or do I just not like the look of it? Sometimes the line between 'weed' and 'wildflower' is thinner than you think.

WHY WEEDS ARE SO GOOD AT SURVIVING

Weeds are survivors. That's why they drive us mad. They've evolved to germinate fast, grow quickly and spread like wildfire. Some spread by seed (think dandelion spores floating across the lawn); others by underground runners (hello, bindweed); and some by deep roots that snap if you so much as look at them (dock, I'm looking at you).

The key to tackling weeds is to understand how they grow and then outsmart them. You don't need chemicals (I never use them myself), just persistence, timing and a few tricks up your sleeve.

PREVENTION BEATS CURE

The best way to deal with weeds is to stop them getting started. A bare patch of soil is basically an open invitation. Seeds blow in, land, and before you know it, they've set up home. So your first weapon is cover.

- **Mulch** – As we covered in the last section, mulch is brilliant for suppressing weeds. A 5cm layer of compost, bark or leaf mould blocks the light that weeds need to germinate.
- **Ground cover plants** – Low-growing perennials, like geraniums, creeping thyme or lamium, spread out and leave no room for weeds to sneak in. Think of them as the garden's 'bouncers'.
- **Dense planting** – Pack your borders with plants that knit together. Gaps between plants are prime weed real estate.

In other words, if you don't want to spend all summer weeding, focus on filling the soil with something useful before weeds do it for you.

THE RIGHT TOOL FOR THE JOB

Forget pulling weeds out with your bare hands (unless you enjoy sore fingers). The right tool makes the job ten times easier.

- **Hand fork or trowel** – Perfect for small weeds in borders or pots. Get under the roots and lift them out whole.
- **Long-handled hoe** – My go-to for veg beds and gravel paths. You just skim it across the soil surface, and it slices weeds off at the base. Quick, easy and oddly satisfying.

- **Lawn weeder** – A brilliant gadget that lets you lever out deep-rooted weeds like dandelions without bending down. You push it into the ground, twist, and out pops the whole root. Magic – and fun.
- **Spring-tine rake** – Great for pulling moss and little weeds out of the lawn while you scarify.

If you've ever tried tackling bindweed or couch grass with just your fingers, you'll know why tools matter. You never get the whole root, and two weeks later it's back, stronger than ever.

TIMING IS EVERYTHING

Weeding is a bit like laundry. Leave it too long, and the pile gets overwhelming. Stay on top of it regularly, and it's manageable.

Weed little and often – Ten minutes a week is better than one exhausting marathon session.

After rain – The best time to weed is when the soil's damp. Roots slip out easily. Try it in dry soil, and you'll just snap the tops off.

Before flowering – Don't let weeds set seed. One dandelion head can scatter hundreds of seeds. If you can't pull it out straight away, at least nip off the flowers before they spread.

I once left a patch of ground elder 'just for a few weeks' while I was busy with other jobs. Big mistake. By the time I got round to it, it had spread like wildfire, and it took me the rest of the season to get it under control. Lesson learned: a little attention early saves you a lot of pain later.

Specific Weed Villains (and How to Handle Them)

Every garden has its 'usual suspects'. Some are easy to pull, others seem designed by nature purely to test your patience. Let's go through the big offenders you'll almost certainly face, and how to deal with them without losing your sanity.

DANDELIONS

What they look like
Rosettes of jagged leaves (they look a bit like lion's teeth, which is where the name comes from), with tall hollow stems and those famous yellow flowers that turn into fluffy seed heads.

Why they're tricky
They have a deep taproot that can stretch down 30cm or more. Snap it off halfway, and the root will just regrow. That's why pulling off the leaves never works long-term.

How to tackle them
Use a long, narrow tool like a weeding knife or lawn weeder to lever out the root. Aim to get the whole thing in one go. If that's not possible, keep weakening the plant by cutting it back before it flowers and spreads seed.

BINDWEED (AKA THE GARDEN STRANGLER)

What it looks like
Pretty white trumpet flowers climbing through your plants. Don't be fooled. It wraps around stems, pulling them down and stealing their light.

Why it's tricky
Underground, it spreads like a spider's web, sending out long white runners that can sprout new shoots metres away from where you first saw it. Break a bit off and it happily regrows.

How to tackle it

There's no quick fix. The best method is persistence. Keep pulling it back as soon as you see it, don't let it flower and carefully dig out runners whenever you can. Over time, repeated attacks weaken it. In my own garden, I've had to treat it like a regular visitor. I don't panic anymore, I just pull and move on.

NETTLES

What they look like

Tall, serrated leaves, often in clumps, with a sting that lets you know if you've brushed past one.

Why they're tricky

They spread by seed *and* creeping underground roots. Leave them unchecked and they'll take over.

How to tackle them

Gloves are essential. Dig them out when the soil is damp, trying to get as much root as possible. The good news? Nettles in a corner of the garden aren't all bad. They're one of the best food plants for butterflies (Peacock and Red Admiral caterpillars, in particular).

COUCH GRASS

What it looks like

To the untrained eye, just grass. But you'll know it's couch when you try to pull it up and find a tough, white, rope-like root (called a rhizome) spreading everywhere.

Why it's tricky

Every tiny bit of root left in the soil will regrow. It's relentless.

How to tackle it

Patience and persistence. Dig it out thoroughly, shaking off as much soil as possible, and be prepared to repeat the process several times. It's not a one-and-done job, but every removal session weakens the plant.

CHICKWEED

What it looks like
Low-growing, fresh green, with tiny, white, star-shaped flowers. Looks innocent, but don't underestimate it.

Why it's tricky
It seeds like crazy. A single plant can produce thousands of seeds, and they germinate in days.

How to tackle it
Hoe it off when it's small, before it flowers. On bare soil, a quick hoeing once a week keeps it down. If it gets away from you, pull it out by hand before it scatters seed everywhere.

DOCK

What they look like
Large, broad leaves, often with tall spikes of reddish-brown seeds in summer.

Why they're tricky
They have a deep taproot, like dandelions, only thicker and harder to remove. They also self-seed freely if left to flower.

How to tackle them
Get them when they're young, before the root gets too deep. If you're dealing with a big one, dig it out after rain when the soil is softer. You might not always get the whole root, but repeated digging weakens it.

HORSETAIL (EQUISETUM)

What it looks like
It starts with little upright shoots that look like asparagus, then grows into tall, wiry stems with bottle-brush-like fronds. Honestly, it looks like something from prehistoric times, which makes sense, because it is. Horsetail has been around since the dinosaurs.

Why it's tricky
Where do I start? The roots can go down several metres. Yes, metres. Break a bit off and it regrows. Cut the top and it shrugs it off. And it spreads underground with a vast network of rhizomes. If you've got horsetail, you'll know why some gardeners call it 'the immortal weed'.

How to tackle it
The brutal truth: you can't get rid of horsetail overnight. Anyone who tells you otherwise is lying. But you can control it. Here's how:
- **Keep cutting it down** as soon as it appears. Don't let it photosynthesise, and over time, the root system weakens.
- **Improve your soil.** Horsetail thrives in poor, compacted ground. Adding compost, mulching and aerating helps tip the balance in favour of your other plants.
- **Don't rotavate it.** All you'll do is chop up the roots and create hundreds more plants.
- **Use dense planting or mulching** to smother it. It hates competition.
- **Accept it may be a long-term battle.** In my experience, the aim isn't eradication but control, keeping it weak enough that your chosen plants thrive while horsetail sulks in the background.

Every weed has its own survival trick. Deep roots, fast seeds, underground runners. That's why there's no 'one method fits all'. The key is learning how each one works and then turning its strengths against it.

Dandelions and docks? Go for the roots.
Chickweed? Stop it seeding.
Bindweed? Persistence and pulling.
Horsetail? Smother, cut back and improve the soil.

You'll never have a completely weed-free garden, and honestly, you don't need one. The aim isn't perfection. It's balance. Keep the weeds in check, give your plants the advantage, and the whole garden will look after itself.

My 'Weeding Without the Pain' Tricks

Over the years, I've learned a few hacks that make weeding less of a chore:

1. **Use a kneeling pad or stool** – Your knees and back will thank you. I resisted for years because I thought it looked 'too serious', but now I wouldn't be without one.
2. **Do it in short bursts** – Ten minutes with a hoe in the evening is more enjoyable than an all-day slog.
3. **Listen to music or a podcast** – Makes the time fly. I've had some of my best ideas while weeding to a good playlist.
4. **Make it social** – My kids love 'weed races': who can fill a bucket the fastest? (Yes, I have definitely let them win sometimes.)
5. **Don't chase perfection** – Aim for 'good enough', not 'Chelsea Flower Show'. A few weeds left behind won't ruin your garden.

ACCEPTING A LITTLE MESS

Here's the controversial bit: you don't actually have to remove every weed.

Some weeds feed pollinators. Dandelions, clover and nettles are all brilliant for bees and butterflies. A bit of 'messy gardening' can actually make your garden healthier and more alive. The trick is balance. Keep weeds under control in the areas where they'll cause problems (like veg beds or paths), but don't feel you have to wage total war everywhere.

I've got a patch at the back of my garden that I deliberately leave a bit wild. Nettles, clover and even the odd dock are allowed to do their thing. In return, I get butterflies, bees and plenty of wildlife. It's not untidy, it's intentional. That little mindset shift makes all the difference.

The Bottom Line on Weeds

Weeds are part of gardening. They're not a sign you've failed, they're just a reminder that nature doesn't wait for us to catch up. The trick is to stay one step ahead without letting them take over your weekends.

Mulch where you can, plant densely, use the right tools and weed little and often. And when you do tackle them, remember it doesn't have to be perfect. A few weeds here and there won't ruin your garden, in fact, they might even make it richer for the wildlife.

Weeding is one of those jobs that feels never-ending, but every time you pull one out, you're tipping the balance in favour of the plants you want. And over time, that adds up to a garden that's healthier, calmer and a lot less stressful.

I used to think every bed had to be weed-free, every edge crisp, every leaf cleared. But the more I've gardened, the more I've realised that perfection is exhausting and nature doesn't work that way anyway. Wild gardens thrive in their own glorious chaos. And the truth? Allowing a bit of that mess into your space can actually *help* your plants and wildlife.

Messy Tips

MESS FEEDS THE SOIL

Those fallen leaves you're tempted to bag up and chuck, they're gold dust. Left in borders, they break down and turn into leaf mould, which enriches your soil. Old stems and plant matter also add organic material that improves soil structure.

So, instead of stressing about getting every last leaf off the ground, think of it this way: you're making dinner for your soil. Mulch, compost and natural debris all return nutrients to the earth.

MESS SHELTERS WILDLIFE

That pile of twigs you were going to burn? It could be a five-star hotel for hedgehogs. A stack of hollow stems left standing over winter? Perfect hiding spots for ladybirds and lacewings. Even leaving a corner of the lawn long gives insects and frogs a chance to thrive.

Wildlife doesn't live in neat, sterile gardens. It lives in nooks, crannies and mess. And those creatures, in turn, help *you* by eating pests, pollinating flowers and generally keeping the garden ecosystem ticking.

MESS PROTECTS PLANTS

Those floppy stems and seed heads you didn't cut back act as little frost guards for the soil beneath, protecting plant crowns and keeping things warmer over winter. Tall ornamental grasses and plants like echinacea look beautiful dusted with frost, but they also help shield less hardy plants nearby.

Think of it as your plants giving each other blankets. Cutting everything down to bare soil in autumn might look tidy, but it leaves plants exposed and vulnerable.

MESS MAKES LESS WORK FOR YOU

This one's simple: if you stop chasing a 'perfect' garden, you save yourself hours of unnecessary work. Do you *really* need to pick up every single leaf off the border? No. Does every weed have to come out immediately? Not unless it's going to seed everywhere. Gardening is meant to be enjoyable, not a constant battle.

I like to call this the 'good enough' rule. Tidy enough that the garden feels cared for, but messy enough that it's still alive and interesting.

MESS CAN BE BEAUTIFUL

This is the part people forget. A seed head silhouetted against the winter sun is stunning. Frosted grass stems swaying in January look far more magical than bare earth. A slightly wild border often has more charm than a rigid one.

Some of my favourite moments in the garden have been messy ones: watching finches perch on dried echinacea heads, or seeing kids kick through leaf piles I'd 'forgotten' to clear.

WHERE TO BE MESSY (AND WHERE NOT TO BE)

Mess works best in some areas, less so in others. Here's the balance I've found:
- **Good messy** = borders, wildlife corners, compost heaps, piles of leaves, seed heads, ornamental grasses left standing.
- **Bad messy** = paths (slippy leaves are dangerous), veg patches (weeds compete with crops), gutters (blocked drains cause real problems).

So, tidy where it matters for safety or productivity, and relax everywhere else.

Don't let tidiness become the enemy of joy. Messy gardening doesn't mean lazy gardening, it means working with nature instead of against it. Your soil, your plants and your wildlife will thank you. And best of all, you'll spend more time enjoying the garden instead of chasing impossible perfection.

Conclusion: Finding Balance in the Chaos

Mulching, weeding and tidying – on paper, these sound like the 'chores' of gardening. The unglamorous jobs nobody rushes outside to do. But the truth is, they're the backbone of a healthy garden. Mulch feeds the soil and keeps plants strong. Weeding clears the way for the plants you actually want. And a bit of tidying keeps everything safe and manageable.

But – and this is important – none of this has to be perfect. Gardens aren't meant to look like showrooms. They're meant to be alive. A dandelion or two doesn't make you a bad gardener. A pile of leaves left for the hedgehogs isn't laziness, it's kindness. And if you don't get around to mulching every border in one weekend, that's fine. A little and often is far more sustainable than trying to blitz everything.

Find that balance: some areas of your garden will be neat, mulched and weed-free; others will be wilder, feeding the soil and sheltering wildlife. And somewhere in the middle is the sweet spot, a garden that feels cared for, but still natural.

So, next time you're out there with your rake, trowel or bucket of mulch, remember this: you're not just tidying; you're setting the stage for stronger plants, healthier soil and a garden that will reward you ten times over. And if you leave a messy corner along the way, even better. That's where the magic often happens.

10
PRUNING AND DEADHEADING

I've touched on pruning a fair bit in the seasonal chapters, but this chapter goes into more detail and will give you all the advice you need if you've not done it before or want more pointers.

Here's what I want you to remember as we dive in: pruning isn't scary. It's not a mysterious art reserved for expert gardeners in tweed jackets. It's just plant maintenance with scissors. And once you know the basics like what to cut, when to cut and what to leave alone, it becomes one of the most satisfying jobs in the garden.

There's something incredibly therapeutic about it too. A few minutes snipping away, clearing out the dead wood, shaping a plant back into balance, it clears your head as much as it clears the garden.

The one mistake I see people make more than anything else is cutting at the wrong time of year. That's the thing that really knocks plants back. Get the timing roughly right, and the technique doesn't have to be perfect. Get the timing wrong, and you might accidentally chop off the very buds that were going to flower. That's when you end up with a hydrangea that sulks all summer or a wisteria that refuses to bloom. So you can avoid this, I've given you a handy seasonal pruning calendar at the end of the chapter, which should take away all the guesswork.

So take a breath, grab your secateurs and don't worry about making it perfect. By the end of this chapter, you'll not only know how to prune and deadhead confidently, but you'll probably start to enjoy it. Who knows, you might even become one of those gardeners (like me) who secretly looks forward to a good pruning session!

Why Pruning Feels Scary (But Shouldn't)

If there's one gardening job that strikes fear into the hearts of beginners, it's pruning. You hand someone a trowel, and they'll happily dig. A watering can? No problem. But pass over a pair of secateurs and say, 'Right, time to prune,' and suddenly you see panic in their eyes. The thought is always the same, *'What if I cut the wrong bit and kill the plant?'*

Trust me, I get it. My first attempts at pruning were a mix of hesitation and mild butchery. I'd stand in front of a rose bush for twenty minutes, secateurs in hand, convinced that one wrong snip would doom it forever. Then I'd finally cut something, usually the wrong thing, and spend the next week worrying that I'd committed some horticultural crime. Spoiler: the rose didn't die. In fact, it grew back better than before, because here's the secret nobody tells you: plants are tougher and more forgiving than you think.

Pruning isn't about perfection. It's about giving your plants a bit of guidance, like tidying a fringe that's grown over someone's eyes. Too long, and it's a mess. Too short, and it looks a bit silly, but it grows back anyway. Most plants are exactly the same. Even if you prune a bit too hard, they usually bounce back with fresh growth.

The truth is, pruning is a powerful exercise in gardening. Done right, it:

Encourages healthier, stronger growth.
Produces more flowers and fruit.
Prevents plants from getting overcrowded or straggly.
Keeps everything looking neat, rather than wild and unruly.

And yet, here's the funny bit, nature doesn't prune. No one's out there giving wild rudbeckia a chop or cutting back a hydrangea in perfect style. Left alone, plants get on just fine. But in our gardens, we prune because we want them to perform in a certain way. More flowers, better shape, fewer tangles.

So, while it isn't always essential, it is the crucial difference between 'surviving' plants and 'thriving' ones. Pruning is confidence-building as much as plant-shaping. The more you do it, the less you'll fear it.

The Basics: How to Prune Without Ruining Your Plants

Here's the golden truth about pruning: most of the fear is in your head. Plants are not fragile snowflakes. They are survivors. They've been nibbled by rabbits, battered by storms, and they keep coming back. Your secateurs aren't going to finish them off.

The trick is to understand *why* you're cutting, not just *where*. Pruning isn't about randomly chopping until the plant looks smaller (though, let's be honest, that's how many of us start). It's about encouraging healthy growth, better flowers and a plant that fits nicely into your space. Here's your guide to pruning without stress.

STEP 1: KNOW WHAT YOU'RE DEALING WITH

Different plants have different pruning needs. Roses aren't pruned the same way as hydrangeas. Wisterias aren't pruned like fruit trees. So, before you start snipping, do a little check.

Ask yourself:
- Is it a shrub, a climber, a tree, or a perennial?
- Does it flower on old wood (last year's growth) or new wood (this year's growth)?

Quick rule of thumb:
- If it flowers in spring, prune it *after* flowering (because the buds were set the year before).
- If it flowers in summer or autumn, prune it in winter or early spring (because it flowers on new growth).

Get that basic principle down, and you'll avoid 90% of pruning disasters.

STEP 2: START WITH THE 3 D'S

This is the easiest way to start pruning, and you can't go wrong. Cut these out first, and you've already improved the health of the plant:
- **Dead wood** – brown, brittle stems that snap easily.
- **Damaged wood** – stems that are broken or split.
- **Diseased wood** – anything blackened, mouldy, or looking suspicious.

STEP 3: OPEN IT UP

Plants need air and light, just like us. For some shrubs, especially roses, gooseberries, currants and certain ornamental shrubs, the best approach is to open up the centre, so sunlight and air can circulate. If the middle looks like a tangled bird's nest, thin it out. Remove stems that cross over each other or rub together, because they can cause wounds where disease sneaks in. The goal with these plants is a shape a bit like a bowl, with strong stems around the outside and an airy, uncluttered middle.

But not every shrub wants this treatment. Some, like lilacs or forsythia (a shrub with star-shaped yellow flowers), prefer a more natural bushy habit, so instead of hollowing out the middle, you simply take out the oldest stems at the base to keep the plant fresh and vigorous. Evergreen shrubs (like box or holly) are different again: they're usually pruned just for shape, not for light and air in the middle.

Think of it like tidying a house. Some spaces need a full clear-out so everything flows smoothly (that's your bowl-shaped shrubs). Others just need you to occasionally swap out the old furniture and keep things ticking along. The trick is knowing which is which, and once you do, pruning feels a lot less scary.

STEP 4: CUT ABOVE A BUD

When you make a cut, do it just above a bud (the little bump where new growth comes from), at a slight angle, so rain runs off. The bud should point in the direction you want the new growth to go (usually outwards, not into the centre of the plant). That way, you're not just removing, you're guiding the plant's next move.

STEP 5: DON'T BE SCARED TO CUT HARDER THAN YOU THINK

This is the bit that freaks beginners out. You make one cut, step back, panic and decide that's enough. But many plants respond brilliantly to a proper haircut. Roses, for example, flower better when pruned back hard. Some shrubs (like buddleia) can be cut almost to the ground in spring and will rocket back up with fresh growth.

STEP 6: KEEP YOUR TOOLS SHARP

Blunt secateurs crush stems instead of slicing cleanly, leaving ragged wounds that take longer to heal (and invite disease). Keep a sharpening stone or even just a bit of sandpaper handy. Sharp tools = healthier cuts.

STEP 7: STEP BACK AND LOOK

Don't just prune with your head down in the branches. Step back every so often and look at the overall shape. The best pruning balances health with aesthetics. You're aiming for a plant that looks natural, not like it got hacked by Edward Scissorhands.

Bottom line, pruning isn't about perfection. It's about health, space and guidance. If you follow the 3 D's, cut just above buds and remember the old wood/new wood rule, you won't go far wrong. And if you do make a mistake? Don't panic. Plants forgive. By next season, you'll barely notice.

Deadheading: The Secret to Longer Blooms

If pruning is the serious, structural part of gardening, deadheading is the easy, everyday version. Think of it as tidying up your plants so they keep performing instead of giving up early.

Here's the deal: plants only have one mission in life, to reproduce. Flowers are their way of attracting pollinators so they can set seed. Once a flower dies and the seed pods form, the plant thinks, 'Job done. No need to waste energy on more flowers.'

Deadheading is simply tricking the plant into carrying on. By snipping or pinching off faded blooms, you stop seeds forming and send a clear message, *'Not done yet, keep going!'* The result? More flowers, for longer.

WHY DEADHEADING MATTERS

- **Keeps plants looking tidy** – No one wants a border full of brown, shrivelled blooms.
- **Encourages repeat flowering** – Many plants will produce a fresh flush if you remove the old heads.
- **Redirects energy** – Instead of wasting strength on seeds, the plant pumps resources into more growth and more flowers.

It's the simplest job in gardening with the biggest payoff. Honestly, if you only do one thing in summer, make it deadheading.

HOW TO DEADHEAD

1. **Find the faded flower** – It'll look brown, floppy, or just past its best.
2. **Follow the stem down** – Don't just pinch the top, trace the stem back to a healthy set of leaves or a side bud.
3. **Snip or pinch** – Cut just above that bud or leaf joint. If the stem is soft, you can even pinch with your fingers.
4. **Repeat, repeat, repeat** – Make it a small daily habit. The more you do it, the more flowers you'll get.

PLANTS THAT LOVE DEADHEADING

- **Roses** – Snip faded blooms down to the first strong leaf set (usually five leaflets). Keeps them flowering all summer.
- **Dahlias** – A classic deadheading plant. Always remove the spent flower head *and* its little swollen base (that's a seed pod). Otherwise, the plant stops producing.
- **Cosmos** – These airy, daisy-like flowers just keep coming if you keep picking or deadheading.
- **Marigolds** – Snip off faded orange heads and they'll bounce back with more colour.
- **Geraniums (*pelargoniums*)** – Twist or cut the whole flower stalk once the cluster is fading.

If you're not sure whether a flower is spent or about to open, give it a gentle squeeze. Buds are firm, spent blooms are soft and papery.

And if in doubt? Deadhead it anyway. The plant won't mind.

Deadheading is gardening's easiest hack. No fancy tools, no complicated techniques, just a few snips here and there and suddenly your plants are blooming twice as long as before.

WHEN TO STOP DEADHEADING

Deadheading can go on all summer and into autumn, but there comes a point when you let the plant rest. Towards the end of the season (September/October), you might want to leave the last few seed heads for wildlife or for collecting seed yourself. Plants like sunflowers, echinacea and rudbeckia produce seed heads that birds adore in winter.

So think of deadheading as a balance. Keep cutting for more flowers through the peak season, then let a few go to seed at the end to feed the garden's wildlife.

Here's the bit most people forget: deadheading isn't just about aesthetics; it's about creating a rhythm in the garden. That small, regular act of snipping connects you to your plants. It gets you looking closely at buds, leaves and stems. You'll often spot pests, diseases or even weeds while you're deadheading – things you'd have missed otherwise.

For me, it's also therapeutic. Ten minutes deadheading after a shift at the fire station feels like clearing my own head. It's repetitive, calming, and the payoff is both instant (tidier beds) and long-term (weeks more colour).

Common Pruning Mistakes (and How to Avoid Them)

Here's the truth: most plants don't die because you forgot to prune them. They die because someone pruned them at the wrong time, in the wrong way, or with the wrong tool. And the number one mistake? Cutting with confidence when you don't quite know what you're cutting.

Don't worry – I've made every mistake in the book. I've cut roses to stumps, trimmed hydrangeas too early and once gave a wisteria such a severe haircut that it sulked for two years before flowering again. So, think of this section as me saving you from my own disasters.

MISTAKE 1: PRUNING AT THE WRONG TIME

This is the big one. Pruning at the wrong time of year is like showing up to the cinema after the credits have rolled – you've missed the moment.

- **Spring-flowering shrubs** (like forsythia, lilac or camellia) bloom on *last year's wood*. If you prune them in winter or early spring, you're literally cutting off the buds that would have flowered. Always prune these straight after they've finished flowering.
- **Summer- and autumn-flowering plants** (like buddleia, roses or *hydrangea paniculata*) bloom on *this year's new growth*. These can be pruned hard in late winter or early spring without losing flowers.

MISTAKE 2: CUTTING TOO HARD (OR NOT HARD ENOUGH)

Some gardeners are too timid, they make tiny snips that barely change the plant. Others (like me in my early days) go full 'Edward Scissorhands' and hack things back to nothing.

- **Too light** = plant gets leggy, overcrowded and messy.
- **Too hard** = you risk shocking or even killing it (especially if you chop off all the buds).

The balance is to cut back enough to shape the plant and encourage fresh growth, but always leave healthy buds or shoots to grow from.

MISTAKE 3: BLUNT OR DIRTY TOOLS

This one doesn't sound glamorous, but it's vital. A blunt pair of secateurs doesn't cut, it tears. That leaves ragged wounds that heal slowly, making plants more prone to disease. Dirty blades can spread fungal spores or bacteria from one plant to the next.

Keep secateurs sharp and clean. A quick wipe with soapy water or disinfectant after use is all it takes. Your plants will thank you.

MISTAKE 4: IGNORING THE '3 DS'

Before you get fancy with shaping, always start with the basics: cut out the **dead**, **damaged** and **diseased wood**. This clears the way for healthy growth and reduces problems down the line.

MISTAKE 5: FORGETTING THE PLANT'S NATURAL SHAPE

Every plant has a natural form: some are vase-shaped, some are rounded, some are tall and upright. A common mistake is forcing them into shapes they don't suit. You don't want a square hydrangea or a ball-shaped wisteria.

Instead of fighting the plant, work with its natural growth habit. Gentle guidance looks better and is easier for the plant.

MISTAKE 6: FEAR OF MAKING MISTAKES

Yes, this is a mistake in itself. Loads of beginners avoid pruning altogether because they're terrified of 'ruining' a plant. But here's the good news: most plants are tougher than you think. Even if you cut back too hard, they'll usually recover with time.

Early on, I cut my *hydrangea macrophylla* (the mophead type) right down in March, thinking I was being clever. That year we didn't get a single flower because I'd snipped off every single bud that had formed the previous autumn. Did the plant die? No. The leaves came back fine, and the next year it flowered again. But I learned the hard way that timing is everything.

Avoid these six mistakes, and you're already ahead of most gardeners. Keep your cuts clean, time them right, respect the plant's shape and don't let fear hold you back.

The Chelsea Chop Explained

The 'Chelsea chop' might sound like a fancy haircut, but don't worry – you don't need to book an appointment or buy hairdressing scissors. It's simply a gardening technique for pruning back certain perennials (plants that come back every year) in late May. It's called the Chelsea chop because that's usually when the Chelsea Flower Show takes place – a good reminder in the calendar of when to do it.

So, what is it?
In plain terms, the Chelsea chop is just cutting back some of your perennial plants by about a third to a half in late spring. You don't chop them down to the ground, you're just giving them a little trim. It might feel a bit brutal at first, but trust me, the plants bounce back stronger than ever.

Why do gardeners do it?
- **It makes plants bushier.** When you cut back the top growth, the plant sends out more side shoots, which means a fuller, sturdier plant instead of something tall and floppy.
- **It extends flowering.** Chopped stems flower a few weeks later than the untouched ones. If you only chop half a plant (or just some of your plants), you'll get flowers spread out over a longer time, rather than everything blooming in one big rush.
- **It prevents flopping.** Tall plants like sedum, rudbeckia and phlox can sometimes fall over under their own weight. Cutting them back keeps them more compact and upright.

HOW TO DO IT (STEP-BY-STEP)

1. **Choose your plant** – Good candidates include sedum (ice plant), phlox, rudbeckia, echinacea, asters and helenium.
2. **Decide how much to chop** – Use clean secateurs and snip the top third to half of the plant's growth. Don't cut lower than where you see strong healthy leaves.
3. **All or some?** – You can chop the whole clump to compact it, or just half so you get two waves of blooms – early ones on the uncut stems and later ones on the cut stems.

4. **Aftercare** – Water if the soil is dry, and that's it. The plant will soon shoot up fresh growth and reward you later in the season.

In my garden, I sometimes 'half-chop' my sedums. The uncut ones flower in early autumn, while the chopped stems flower a bit later. The result? My border has colour for much longer, instead of everything peaking and fading at the same time.

PLANTS THAT RESPOND WELL TO THE CHELSEA CHOP

Here are some reliable perennials that take the Chelsea chop in their stride:
- **Sedum** – Becomes sturdier, less floppy and flowers later.
- ***Phlox paniculata*** – Bushier growth, flowers spread over weeks instead of one big flush.
- **Rudbeckia (Black-eyed Susan)** – Stays compact and upright.
- **Echinacea (Coneflower)** – More side shoots, so more flowers.
- **Aster (Michaelmas daisy)** – Tidy habit and extended blooming.
- **Helenium** – Flowers later in the season, keeping borders colourful.
- **Nepeta (Catmint)** – A lighter chop encourages fresh new growth and more flowers.

PLANTS TO AVOID CHOPPING

Not every plant enjoys being cut back this way. Don't Chelsea chop:
- **Roses** – They have their own pruning schedule (see pages 187–8).
- **Woody shrubs** – This technique is only for herbaceous perennials.
- **Delicate perennials** that flower early in the season (like peonies) – you'll lose this year's show.

The Chelsea chop isn't essential, but it's a brilliant little trick if you've got tall perennials that get leggy or if you want to spread out your flowering season. Think of it as pressing 'pause' on part of the plant to save the show for later.

In Detail: Hydrangeas, Roses and Wisteria

Some plants forgive anything. You can hack them back, cut them at the wrong time, and they'll shrug it off. But others are fussier. Cut them wrong, and you'll be staring at a lot of leaves and no flowers for an entire year.

Hydrangeas, roses and wisteria fall into this 'high maintenance but worth it' category. Get them right, and they'll reward you with some of the most spectacular displays in any garden. Get them wrong, and... well, let's just say I've had summers with very leafy, very flowerless shrubs.

First things first: what's a bud?

If you're new to gardening, the word *bud* gets thrown around a lot. A bud is basically a plant's 'new bit in waiting'. It's a little swollen bump on a stem that will grow into either a leaf or a flower.

- **Leaf buds** are usually slimmer and pointed, often sitting along the sides of stems.
- **Flower buds** tend to be fatter and rounder, especially on shrubs like hydrangeas.

When pruning, the advice is often to 'cut above a bud'. That just means don't leave long stubs of stem, cut just above one of those little bumps. The plant then sends energy into that bud, which shoots off into new growth. Simple once you know what you're looking for.

HYDRANGEAS

Hydrangeas can be confusing because there are several types, and they don't all behave the same way. Before pruning, you need to know which one you've got.

- **Mophead and Lacecap hydrangeas (*Hydrangea macrophylla*)**
  – *What they look like* – Mopheads have big, round pompom flowers (like giant scoops of ice cream). Lacecaps have flat flower heads with tiny fertile flowers in the middle, surrounded by a ring of larger, showy ones.
  – *How they flower* – On old wood. The stems made the year before.
  – *How to prune* – In spring, just remove last year's dried flower heads. Cut just above a pair of healthy fat buds lower down the stem. Don't cut them all the way back or you'll lose that year's flowers.

- *Beginner trap* – Cutting back too hard in spring. You'll end up with a healthy green bush and no blooms.
- **Hydrangea paniculata (like 'Limelight') and *arborescens* (like 'Annabelle')**
  – *What they look like* – Paniculata types have big, cone-shaped flower heads. Arborescens types (like the famous 'Annabelle') have large, round white heads that can be as big as a football.
  – *How they flower* – On new wood. Fresh stems made the same year.
  – *How to prune* – In late winter or early spring, cut them back hard to about 30–40cm above the ground. It looks savage, but don't panic – they'll throw up strong new shoots and bloom like crazy.

If your hydrangea has cone-shaped flowers, it's almost certainly a paniculata and safe to prune hard. If it's a round mophead, treat it gently.

ROSES

Roses strike fear into beginners because there are so many 'rules'. But in reality, roses are tough plants. They'll survive even if your cuts aren't perfect. The key is understanding the main types and what they need.

- **Hybrid Teas**
  – *What they look like* – Classic long-stemmed roses, usually with one flower per stem (think florist roses).
  – *How to prune* – In late winter/early spring, cut stems back by about a third to half. Always cut just above an outward-facing bud (so growth goes outwards, not inwards where it'll tangle).
- **Floribundas**
  – *What they look like* – Bushier than hybrid teas, with clusters of flowers on each stem.
  – *How to prune* – Similar approach and again in late winter/early spring. Shorten the stems by about a third and thin out any congested growth.
- **Shrub Roses**
  – *What they look like* – Bigger, bushier plants, often old-fashioned varieties with masses of flowers.
  – *How to prune* – These don't need precision. Just thin out older stems to keep air moving and cut back the rest by about a third. Aim for around February to March to do this.

- **Climbing Roses**
  – *What they look like* – Long, arching stems that need support against walls, fences or arches.
  – *How to prune* – The trick is to tie in new stems **horizontally**, as that's what makes them flower all along the shoot. Then, cut out older, woody stems at the base. These need tackling after they have flowered, usually around August. If you have a repeat flowering rose, aim for early spring.

How to tell roses apart if you're unsure:
- If it's trained on a wall, fence or arch, it's probably a climber.
- If it has single blooms per stem, it's likely a hybrid tea.
- If it has clusters, you're probably looking at a floribunda.
- If it's sprawling into a big shrub, treat it as a shrub rose.

With any rose, remove dead, diseased or crossing stems first. After that, shorten and shape. Don't overthink it.

WISTERIA

Wisteria is the plant that makes people dream of country cottages, with purple waterfalls of flowers in May and June. But it has a reputation. If you don't prune, it goes wild with greenery and gives you hardly any flowers.
- **Summer prune (July/August)** – Cut back the long whippy shoots to about 5–6 leaves. This reins in the chaos and pushes energy into flower bud formation.
- **Winter prune (January/February)** – Go back and shorten those same shoots again, this time to 2–3 buds. This neatens the framework and sets the stage for flowering.

Wisteria is vigorous and forgiving once you get into the rhythm. Think of it as giving the plant structure. Without pruning, it's unruly. With it, you get the jaw-dropping flowers everyone wants.

Seasonal Pruning Calendar

As I've said before, the timing of when you prune matters a lot. Cut at the wrong time, and you can literally chop off next year's flowers before they even get a chance. Cut at the right time, and you'll encourage healthier growth, bigger blooms and plants that don't look like they've been through a hedge backwards.

To make life easier, here's a **month-by-month pruning guide**. Remember to look back over your seasonal checklist too!

WINTER (DECEMBER–FEBRUARY)

This is when the garden is bare, so you can really see the structure of plants. Growth has slowed right down, so you're less likely to stress plants by pruning now.

- **Apple and Pear Trees** – Prune while dormant. Aim for an open, goblet shape to let in light and air. Remove crossing branches and thin out crowded growth.
- **Wisteria** – In January/February, shorten the summer's long whippy shoots to 2–3 buds. This keeps flowering spurs close to the main framework.
- **Group 3 Clematis** (flower on new growth in late summer, see page 191) – Chop back hard to 30cm above ground in February/March. Looks brutal, but it works.
- **Roses** (hard pruning for hybrid teas and floribundas) – Late winter is great, but early spring will also work. Cut back to 3–5 strong buds, shaping the plant as you go.
- *Hydrangea paniculata* – Cut hard to 30–40cm above ground in late winter or early spring.

SPRING (MARCH–MAY)

Everything's waking up, but don't get carried away. This is gentle pruning season – tidying more than chopping.

- **Group 2 Clematis** (flowers twice in spring and summer, see page 191) – In March, prune lightly, just removing dead or weak stems. Keep the framework intact for that first flush of flowers.
    - *Hydrangea macrophylla* **(Bigleaf hydrangea)** – Don't cut everything! Just remove dead flower heads to the first strong bud.

- **Shrubs that flower in late summer** (like buddleia or fuchsia) – Cut back hard in March/April. They flower on new growth.
- **Fruit bushes** (blackcurrants, gooseberries) – Tidy in early spring before growth kicks off. Remove dead wood and thin the centre.
- **Roses** – Follow the same principle as the winter prune in early spring.

SUMMER (JUNE–AUGUST)

This is when many plants are in full bloom, so pruning is more about maintenance and deadheading to keep the show going.

- **Wisteria** (second prune) – In July/August, cut back the new, whippy green shoots to 5–6 leaves. This channels energy into flower bud production.
- **Roses** – Keep deadheading throughout summer to encourage repeat blooms. Cut back to just above a strong leaf.
- **Lavender** – After flowering (July/August), shear lightly to maintain a neat shape. Don't cut into old, woody stems.
- **Group 1 Clematis** (flowers early on old wood) – Prune just after flowering (usually May/June). These bloom on old wood, so cutting later removes next year's flowers.

AUTUMN (SEPTEMBER–NOVEMBER)

Autumn is the season for tidying and light shaping rather than full-on pruning.

- **Roses** (climbers and ramblers) – Tie in new growth to supports, prune back wayward stems and remove any dead or diseased wood. Save major pruning for late winter.
- **Fruit trees** (stone fruits, like cherry and plum) – If you need to prune, do it in late summer/early autumn, never winter – they're prone to silver leaf disease.
- **Shrubs that have flowered this year** – Cut back lightly to shape.
- **Hedges** – Give them a final trim before growth stops.

Quick Clematis Recap
- **Group 1 (early bloomers like *montana*, *alpina*)**: prune after flowering in spring.
- **Group 2 (big-flowered hybrids)**: light prune in February/March, then tidy again after the first flush in early summer.
- **Group 3 (late bloomers like *viticella*, '*Jackmanii*')**: hard prune in late winter (February/March).

The key thing to remember is flowering time tells you when to prune. If it flowers early, don't prune in winter or you'll lose the buds. If it flowers later in summer, it's usually safe to cut back hard in spring.

Conclusion

Pruning is less about 'rules' and more about learning the rhythm of your plants. Once you get the hang of it, you'll stop second-guessing and start pruning with confidence and your plants will thank you for it with stronger growth and more flowers.

Pruning has a reputation for being complicated, a mysterious art that only seasoned gardeners dare attempt. But, hopefully, by now you can see that it's really not about rules carved in stone. It's about understanding the basics, like what your plant flowers on, when it flowers and how to encourage more of that.

Deadheading keeps things blooming longer. Pruning shapes plants, keeps them healthy and makes sure energy goes where it's needed most. And, yes, the odd mistake happens. We've all lopped off a stem we shouldn't have and winced later. The good news is that most plants are tougher than we give them credit for. They grow back. They forgive.

If you take away one thing from this chapter, let it be this: don't let fear stop you from picking up the secateurs. Plants don't need perfect cuts, they just need you to care enough to give them a trim when they need it. And once you've seen the difference of a rose bursting into more blooms after deadheading, a clematis covered in flowers because you pruned it at the right time, I promise you'll start to enjoy it.

So, sharpen your secateurs, take a deep breath and get stuck in. Don't overthink it. Plants are generous. And the more you practise, the more pruning will become second nature to you.

4

GARDENING WITH KIDS AND FAMILY FUN

11
GROWING TOGETHER
The Family Garden

Gardening doesn't always have to be done solo, it can be a family adventure that brings people together. Whether it's toddlers watering plants, teens helping design your veg patch or parents sharing their wisdom, gardening can offer a space for connection.

In this chapter, I'll give you activities that the whole family can enjoy. Plus, I'll show you some great family projects that work across the seasons, because gardening with kids isn't just about spring sowings, it's about making memories year-round.

GARDENING FOR KIDS: HOW TO GET THEM HOOKED EARLY

If you've ever tried to get kids into gardening, you'll know one thing straight away: they either love it with wild enthusiasm, or they get bored within thirty seconds and wander off to kick a ball instead. And that's fine. Gardening with kids isn't about producing perfect plants, it's about sparking curiosity, giving them a chance to get muddy and letting them feel that wonderful pride of saying, *'I grew this!'*

For me, gardening has always been more than just plants. It's memories. Some of my earliest ones are of being outside, poking around in the soil, nicking strawberries before my mum saw, or 'helping' my Oma (my Dutch grandma) by filling her bucket with far too many weeds. Kids don't remember lectures about soil health. What they remember is the fun, the mess, the sense that the garden was theirs too.

And, honestly, gardening is one of the best gifts you can give to kids. It teaches patience (plants don't grow overnight, no matter how often they check), responsibility (water it or watch it wilt) and resilience (yes, sometimes things die, but you try again). It also gets them off screens, out in the fresh air and connected to the real, living world. In today's world, that's gold dust.

Now, don't worry – you don't need acres of land, fancy tools or even a 'kid-friendly' garden. A few pots, a bag of compost and some seeds are enough to get started. The trick is to make it feel like play, not chores. No lectures about 'doing it properly'. No pressure for perfect results. Just fun, simple tasks that make them feel part of the garden.

Easy, Mess-Friendly Tasks for Little Hands

If there's one thing I've learned from gardening with kids, it's this: forget straight rows, forget clean clothes, forget perfection. Kids don't care if the holes are too big or the seeds are upside down. They just want to 'do' and be with you. And honestly, that's what makes gardening magical for them, and hilarious for you.

Gardening with kids is not about producing prize-winning veg. It's about letting them dig, pour, squish and explore without worrying that they're 'doing it wrong'. The good news? Most kids' natural chaos actually helps. They water too much (great for thirsty seeds), they scatter soil everywhere (hello, free mulching) and they'll proudly plant twenty beans in the same hole (fine, you'll thin them later).

Here are some genuinely easy, mess-friendly tasks that little hands can handle, no matter their age.

1. WATERING DUTY (WITH MINI CANS OR SPRAY BOTTLES)

Give a kid a watering can and you'll soon realise they treat it like a fire hose. Instead of soaking your borders like Noah's flood, set them up with a little child-sized watering can or even a spray bottle. They love the action of squeezing and watching droplets fall.

Top tip: Let them water pots and seed trays. Smaller targets are easier, and they can see instant results (soil darkening, drips coming out of the bottom). In summer, I sometimes hand my kids the job of 'greenhouse spray patrol', where they mist everything like they're playing with a water pistol. Keeps them busy for ages.

2. FILLING SEED TRAYS WITH SOIL

This is basically playing with mud pies, but useful. Give kids a scoop or small trowel and let them fill up seed trays, pots or yoghurt pots with compost. Don't worry if they compact it too much or spill half of it on the patio. You can gently smooth things over when they're not looking.

What's great about this job is the sense of ownership. Kids love the idea that 'this pot is mine', especially if they then get to sow seeds in it and check back every day.

3. DIGGING TINY HOLES

Forget delicate dibbers. Hand kids a stick or a child-sized trowel and let them dig the planting holes for seeds or bulbs. They'll usually make them about three times bigger than needed, but again, that's fine. You can backfill. It's all about giving them the job and letting them feel proud.

And, yes, they'll probably dig random holes where you don't want them, so give them a designated patch of soil where it doesn't matter. Think of it as their 'sandbox of gardening'.

4. COLLECTING TREASURES (LEAVES, STICKS, PETALS)

Kids love collecting. Whether it's conkers, stones or Pokémon cards, it's in their nature. Harness that by asking them to collect 'treasures' from the garden like fallen leaves, twigs, petals, seed pods. They can use them for crafts later (leaf printing, nature collages) or you can chuck the lot on the compost heap. Either way, they feel involved and important.

My youngest once brought me a bucket proudly filled with what he called 'baby sticks'. It was just a pile of twigs. But in his head, he'd saved the garden. That's what it's about: purpose, even if the job itself is simple.

5. PAINTING POTS AND MAKING LABELS

Not every kid wants to dig in the mud. Some love the creative side. Set them up with some old terracotta pots and let them paint faces, stripes, or whatever wild ideas they fancy. Permanent markers or paint pens work too. Scribble monsters, rainbows, or even silly names for the plants ('Dave the Dahlia').

For labels, give them lolly sticks or bits of cardboard and let them decorate. Even if the writing's wobbly, it's theirs. And when they see 'Tomato' in their own handwriting weeks later, they're far more likely to feel connected to what's growing.

6. HARVEST HELPERS

Picking things is the best job for kids. It's instant gratification. Whether it's tugging a carrot out of the ground, popping peas from pods, or hunting for strawberries, they'll be hooked. The trick is letting them pick freely (even if they grab them a bit early). Half the joy is taste-testing straight off the plant.

Top tip: Grow extra of the 'snackable' plants, like peas, strawberries and cherry tomatoes. Kids will eat them before they ever make it to the kitchen, but honestly, that's part of the fun.

7. BUG PATROL

Give kids a magnifying glass and ask them to find creepy crawlies. Worms, beetles, woodlice, it's all exciting. Some kids will proudly adopt a worm and name it; others will run away squealing. Either way, it's an adventure.

You can turn it into a real job by asking them to check under pots for slugs or collect worms for the compost bin. Just don't expect them to be gentle about it!

8. COMPOST 'CHEFS'

Kids love mixing. Show them the compost heap or bin and explain that it's like a giant slow cooker for the garden. They can chuck in veg peelings, leaves, cardboard, and mix it around with a stick. It's messy, slightly smelly and utterly fascinating for them.

The trick with all these jobs is not worrying about mess or perfection. Kids will spill water, sow seeds on top of each other and sometimes pull up your plants by mistake. But that's how they learn. And honestly, it's how they fall in love with gardening, by being allowed to play.

Bring in Snacks and Breaks: Let's be honest, snacks make everything better. Have a stash of biscuits, fruit, or even just juice breaks ready. A 'tea and biscuit break on the patio' or a garden picnic can turn a whiny half hour into another happy hour outside.

End on Fun, Not Work: One of my best tricks? Always finish with something fun. After a weeding session, let the kids water each other with the hose (on a sunny day). After planting, have a race to tidy tools back to the shed. Ending on a laugh makes them want to come back next time.

My son has grown to love gardening, and it's got to the point now where he understands what certain plants need and helps me with the watering when I'm on shift. It's a joy to see.

The Best Plants for Kids to Grow (That Won't Die Overnight)

Here's the deal: if you want kids to stay interested in gardening, you've got to stack the odds in their favour. Nothing kills enthusiasm faster than planting something and then watching it shrivel up two days later because they forgot about it. The secret, start them off with plants that are tough, forgiving and quick to reward their effort.

Think of it like giving a learner driver an old reliable hatchback instead of a McLaren (yes... huge fan). We want plants that will survive a bit of neglect, bounce back from overwatering and look exciting enough to keep their attention.

Here are my tried-and-tested winners:

CRESS – THE CLASSIC STARTER

If gardening for kids had a 'gateway plant', it would be cress. You don't even need soil. Put a bit of damp kitchen paper in an old yoghurt pot, sprinkle seeds on top and within a few days you've got a lush little jungle.

Why it works:
- **Super quick** – germinates in 2–3 days.
- **Edible reward** – they can snip it for sandwiches or salads.
- **Mess-free** – can be grown indoors on a windowsill.
It's instant gratification.

SUNFLOWERS – BIG, BOLD AND BRAG-WORTHY

Sunflowers are the show-offs of the plant world. They grow fast, they grow tall and they make kids feel like they've achieved something epic.

Why they work:
- Big seeds = easy for small hands to plant.
- Grow quickly in warm weather.
- Birds love the seed heads at the end of the season.

Top tip: Plant a couple in large pots near the patio, so kids can measure their progress with a tape measure every week.

ROOT VEGGIES – CARROTS AND RADISHES

Root veg are brilliant because they're hidden underground. Kids love the mystery – you never quite know what's happening until the big reveal when you pull them up.

- **Radishes** – the ultimate quick win. They're ready in just 3–4 weeks. Even if they don't eat them, the excitement of harvesting is worth it.
- **Carrots** – a little slower, but kids love yanking them out of the soil, especially when they come up in funny shapes. Go for shorter varieties ('Paris Market' are small and round, perfect for pots).

Top tip: Plant in pots or raised beds where the soil is light and stone-free.

STRAWBERRIES – SWEET SUCCESS

Strawberries are one of the best kid plants. Why? Because they taste amazing and they're hard to resist. Children will happily water and care for something if they know it ends with a sweet snack.

Why they work:
- Produce fruit in their first year, if you buy young plants.
- Can be grown in pots, hanging baskets or borders.
- The payoff is delicious and instant.

My kids always raid the strawberry patch the second they ripen. Honestly, half the time I don't get any myself, but seeing their excitement makes it worth it.

MARIGOLDS – BRIGHT AND CHEERFUL

Marigolds are virtually indestructible, which makes them perfect for kids. They're colourful, they flower for ages and they don't mind a bit of rough handling.

Why they work:
- Easy to sow from seed.
- Tough as nails (great for forgetful waterers).
- They attract pollinators, so kids get to spot bees and butterflies, too.

SWEET PEAS – FLOWERS YOU CAN PICK

Sweet peas are brilliant for teaching kids that the more you pick, the more they grow. Plus, they smell incredible.

Why they work:
- Easy to grow from seed in pots or the ground.
- Flowers can be cut for little posies. Kids love giving bunches they 'grew themselves.'
- They climb, so you can create little wigwams or teepees for them to grow up.

MINT – TOUGH, TASTY AND FUN

Herbs are great starter plants, and mint is king because it's practically unkillable. Pop it in a pot (always a pot, otherwise it'll spread everywhere) and kids can pick leaves for drinks, teas, or just to rub between their fingers and smell.

COURGETTES – 'MAGIC' PLANTS

Courgette plants are a bit like magic tricks. One day there's nothing, and the next day there's a giant courgette hiding under a leaf. They grow quickly, the flowers are huge and dramatic, and kids love the sense of discovery.

The Golden Rules for Kids' Plants:

1. **Big seeds are best** – easier for little fingers.
2. **Fast results keep attention** – quick germination = quick wins.
3. **Tasty rewards make it real** – grow fruit, veg or herbs they can actually eat.
4. **Forgiving nature** – use plants that won't sulk if they forget to water them for a few days.

If you choose just a handful of the above, you're setting kids up for success. They'll see growth quickly, they'll get hands-on and they'll feel proud when they can eat or show off their plants. And once they've had that buzz, that 'I grew this!' moment, they're hooked for life.

GROWING TOGETHER

Fun Gardening Games and Activities for the Whole Family

Here's the truth: if gardening feels like a 'chore', kids will lose interest fast. But if you turn it into a game, suddenly, it's fun. The good news is that you don't need fancy kits or expensive projects. Most of the best garden activities for kids are simple, messy and powered by imagination.

The Tallest Sunflower Competition
This one's a classic and it works every time. Each family member plants a sunflower seed and measures it weekly. Add a bit of theatre with a tape measure, charts or even a little trophy for the winner. The competition keeps them checking in, and the growth is dramatic enough to wow them.

Seed Bomb Making
Messy? Absolutely. Fun? Even more so. Mix soil, compost and wildflower seeds with a splash of water, roll them into little balls, let them dry and then throw them into bare corners of the garden. Weeks later, you've got wildflowers popping up, and the kids get to feel like real gardeners.

Potato Treasure Hunt
Potatoes are magic for kids because they grow out of sight. When it's time to harvest, get them to dig around with little hands or forks – it's like finding buried treasure. The joy of pulling out handfuls of spuds is unbeatable.

Build a Bug Hotel or Hedgehog Home
Stack sticks, bamboo, bricks or pinecones into a little 'hotel' and tuck it into a corner of the garden. Or pile logs and leaves for hedgehogs. It's creative building and nature-friendly at the same time.

Watering Can Races

If you've got more than one child, give them each a watering can and a patch to water. First one back with an empty can wins. It's chaotic and a bit splashy, but the plants get watered and the kids feel useful. Win-win.

The key with all these games is simple: keep it playful. Don't worry about straight rows or neatness. If seeds get scattered too thickly or a courgette gets overwatered, that's part of the fun. The more joy they have now, the more likely they are to stick with gardening as they grow.

Gardening doesn't have to feel like work. If you lean into the mess, make games of the jobs and drop the pressure for perfection, it becomes family playtime with bonus vegetables and flowers at the end. That's the sweet spot, when the garden gives you memories as well as harvests.

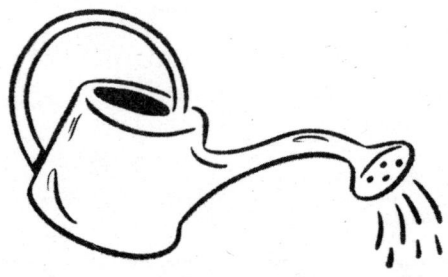

Seasonal Family Gardening: Projects, Play and Simple Wins

For me, the shift into the family getting involved came gradually. At first, gardening was something I did on my own, usually after work when the kids were in bed. But as they got a little older, and as my wife started to see the joy in eating food we'd grown, or having a glass of wine together on the patio surrounded by the blooming dahlias, the garden began to feel like a family room without a ceiling.

So, how do you make gardening a family thing without it feeling like herding cats? One of the best ways to keep the family interested in gardening is to make it seasonal. Instead of trying to cram everything into one big 'gardening day', you can sprinkle little family-friendly jobs throughout the year. It keeps things fresh, gives you all something to look forward to and helps children connect with the rhythm of the seasons. Gardening stops being 'Dad's weird hobby' and becomes part of family life.

SPRING: EXCITEMENT AND NEW BEGINNINGS

Spring is the season of fresh starts, and kids feel that energy too. Everything's waking up, bulbs are pushing through and the soil finally feels alive again.

Family-friendly jobs in spring:

- **Sowing seeds in trays or pots:** Sunflowers, nasturtiums or salad leaves are foolproof. Kids love checking every day to see which pot has sprouted first.
- **Building a simple bug hotel:** Use sticks, pinecones or bricks with holes. Kids get a kick out of 'helping insects move in'.
- **Watering seedlings with a spray bottle:** Small hands struggle with heavy watering cans, so a spray bottle is perfect. Bonus, they won't drown your seedlings.
- **Creating plant labels:** Give kids wooden lolly sticks and paints/markers. Wonky, colourful labels make the veg patch look ten times more fun.

My kids once painted an entire set of plant markers with googly eyes. We ended up with 'Mr Lettuce', 'Captain Sunflower' and 'Queen Carrot'. Did it help with plant ID? Not really. Did it make us laugh every time we walked past? Absolutely.

SUMMER: GROWTH AND HARVEST

Summer can feel like the peak of the gardening year – everything's green, flowers are blooming and veg is coming in fast. For families, it's the most rewarding time because you start seeing results.

Family-friendly jobs in summer:
- **Picking fruit and veg:** Strawberries, raspberries, peas, beans, anything that can be eaten straight from the plant is a hit.
- **Deadheading flowers:** Show kids how to pinch off faded blooms from marigolds or cosmos. It's quick, easy and they see results when more flowers appear.
- **Making daisy chains:** Not everything has to be 'productive'. Sometimes sitting on the lawn making chains is the memory that sticks.
- **Helping to water plants:** On hot days, give kids their own small watering can and a 'patch of responsibility'. Yes, half the water will end up on their shoes, but they'll feel proud.

Top tip: Don't stress if kids over-pick or water too much. A few soggy marigolds or wonky strawberries won't ruin the garden.

AUTUMN: COLLECTING AND PREPARING

Autumn is a brilliant season for kids because it's full of collecting. Seeds, leaves, conkers, apples. Everything feels like treasure.

Family-friendly jobs in autumn:
- **Leaf piles:** Raking isn't a job, it's a game. Get the kids to pile leaves high, then let them dive in.
- **Seed saving:** Sunflower heads, marigold seeds, or peas left to dry are perfect for little fingers to collect and stash.
- **Planting bulbs:** Simple, satisfying and almost magical when flowers appear months later. Show them 'pointy side up' and let them bury a few daffodils or tulips.
- **Pumpkin harvest:** If you grow pumpkins or squash, let the kids pick the biggest one and claim it as their own.

WINTER: REST AND IMAGINATION

Winter isn't about growth, it's about dreaming and small, cosy jobs. The cold doesn't mean you can't involve kids; you just have to adjust.

Family-friendly jobs in winter:
- **Feeding birds:** Filling feeders or cracking ice on the bird bath is a simple way for kids to connect with nature when the garden feels asleep.
- **Making fat balls or seed cakes:** Mix lard, seeds and oats in a bowl, then hang them out. Messy fun that birds love.
- **Planning next year's garden:** Get the kids involved in choosing seeds from catalogues. Warning: you'll end up with way too many sunflowers.
- **Decorating the garden:** Hang homemade bird feeders or fairy lights, or even paint pots ready for spring.

Family Gardening Projects Everyone Can Do

If seasonal jobs are the small wins, family projects are the bigger adventures. These are the things that create memories.
- **Build a raised bed together** – A few planks, some soil, and suddenly you've got a family veg patch. Let the family decide what to grow.
- **Grow a 'pizza garden'** – Plant tomatoes, basil and oregano in a bed or pot. When it's harvest time, you've got homegrown pizza toppings.
- **Create a wildlife corner** – Pile logs, leave leaves, add a small pond (even a washing-up bowl sunk into the ground works). It's great fun checking for frogs, beetles and hedgehogs.
- **Paint and personalise pots** – Terracotta pots + acrylic paint = a Saturday afternoon well spent and could double up as a mindful exercise. Every time you water those plants, you'll see the art. You could also do this with large, smooth stones and use them to decorate parts of the garden.
- **Make it social** – When the weather allows, turn on some music and pour some drinks, even if it's just half an hour after tea spent outside. Even if you just sit and deadhead flowers while chatting. The jobs get done, but more importantly, you're outside, together.

The Partner Factor

I'll be honest, getting your partner involved can be harder than getting the kids on board. Kids are won over with mud and strawberries. Adults need different hooks. For us, food was the winner (along with a glass of wine). The first time my wife harvested her own potatoes and salad leaves and made dinner with them, she was hooked. The goal could be flowers for the house, creating an area of peace and calm, or simply sitting outside with a drink in a space they helped shape. The key is not forcing them into your version of gardening; it's finding the bit that excites them.

Now my wife enjoys a garden potter, deadheading, weeding and watering are all part of the weekly routine, and the enjoyment I get from having the whole family help in some small way is priceless.

Final Thoughts

Gardening with your family isn't about perfection. It's not about neat rows or pristine lawns. It's about mud on shoes, strawberries eaten before they're washed, worms proudly paraded around like pets. It's about giving family members the freedom to explore, make mistakes and learn that sometimes plants die, and that's okay.

If you can spark even a little excitement now, you're planting seeds that last a lifetime. They might not all want to be gardening obsessives, but they'll carry that connection with nature with them. And in a world where screens are everywhere, and connection can be difficult, that's priceless.

So hand them a trowel, let them water until the patio floods and laugh when they pull up your best tulip thinking it's a weed. These are the memories that matter.

Because gardening with family isn't just about the garden. It's about building relationships, bonding, fun and muddy footprints leading back into the house.

5

ASK JONNY

12
YOUR BIGGEST GARDENING QUESTIONS – ANSWERED!

If there's one thing I've learned from sharing my gardening journey online, it's that gardeners are a curious bunch. My inbox and comment sections are always full of questions – everything from *'Why are my hydrangeas sulking?'* to *'Is it normal to spank compost bags?'* (Yes. Absolutely.)

So I thought: why not turn those questions into something bigger? This chapter is dedicated to all of you – the amazing people who have followed, supported, laughed at and occasionally roasted me over the years. Whether you've been here since my very first reel or you stumbled upon me midway through short shorts lawn striping, this section is a thank you. You've made this journey what it is, and it only felt right that you should have a place in the book too.

When I first started posting gardening videos, I never imagined it would turn into a community like this. I was just a bloke in his garden, trying to grow things without killing them and maybe making someone smile along the way. But the questions kept coming, and not just the usual 'how-to' stuff. People asked about gardening for wellbeing, for confidence, for connection. They asked real, honest questions that showed just how much this little hobby means to people.

So I opened it up: across Instagram, TikTok and Facebook, I asked you all to send me your biggest gardening questions, the ones that have been bugging you, confusing you, or keeping you awake at night (because apparently, that's what gardening does to us now). I've chosen a selection to answer here, from the practical to the bizarre. And if your question is included, you might even spot your handle printed right here in black and white!

These questions are real, funny and relatable, and if you've ever made a gardening mistake, don't worry. You're in very good company.

So let's dig in (pun absolutely intended). From the everyday gardening problems to the 'what on earth is this growing in my compost bin?' moments, these are your questions, answered with a healthy dose of honesty, humour and the odd bit of mud.

And if your name's in here – congratulations, you've officially made gardening history! Or at least, you've made it into a book written by a man who wears short shorts in December.

What are your wildlife-friendly solutions for stopping pests getting to your plants?
@melslittlegarden

My go-to approach is to encourage predators. Frogs, birds and hedgehogs eat slugs for fun, so leave a small log pile or dish of water out and they'll do the dirty work for you.

Skip the pellets; they harm more than they help. Use beer traps, copper tape, or even decoy plants like nasturtiums to lure pests away from your favourites. For aphids, I just blast them off with water or squish them (glamorous, I know).

And remember: strong plants resist pests better. Keep them well-fed, watered and spaced out, and they'll bounce back from a few nibbles. Don't aim for perfection; a few holes mean your garden's part of nature, not fighting against it.

If you could only use one tool in your garden, what would it be and why?
@starof_72

Easy, it's got to be the good old-fashioned trowel.

It's the Swiss Army Knife of the garden world. You can dig, plant, weed, scoop compost and even edge a border if you're desperate. I've had the same one for years.

Honestly, if I had to give up all my fancy tools, I'd still be fine with just that trowel. It's the one thing that never lets me down – simple, reliable and always ready to get muddy.

What's your trick to combining colours and textures in plants to make the garden feel balanced?
@marchaldron

Here's how I think about it:

1. Start with texture before colour.
If every plant in your garden has the same leaf shape, it all looks flat. Mix it up with big, bold hosta leaves against fine, feathery ferns; or upright grasses beside low, mound-forming perennials. Texture gives your garden movement even when nothing's flowering.

2. Move on to colour.
Pick a palette rather than every colour under the sun. For a calm feel, go with cool tones: blues, purples, silvers. For energy, use fiery oranges, yellows, reds. My tip? Repeat the same colour in different plants across the garden; it ties everything together, so it looks intentional, not like you tipped out a seed box.

3. Don't forget the green.
People chase flowers, but the magic's in the foliage. Green comes in hundreds of shades and textures – lime, blue-green, dark, matte, glossy – and it's what keeps your garden looking good when blooms fade. I love my shady border – it's full of green and always interesting.

4. Think about seasons, not just summer.
Layer plants that take turns looking good: tulips and alliums for spring; dahlias and grasses for late summer; seed heads and evergreens for winter. A garden that changes through the year feels alive and balanced.

5. Trust your gut.
If something looks right to *you*, it *is* right. Gardening's not interior design with rules, it's about expression.

What's your favourite spring boob?
@greenfingeredcityboy
Ha! Every time I say 'bulb', someone thinks I've gone rogue and started talking about boobs instead. Honestly, I've given up correcting people at this point – just embrace the chaos!

But to answer properly, my favourite spring bulb (yes, bulb!) has to be *Allium* 'Purple Sensation'. Tall, elegant and unapologetically dramatic.

I've just seen your apple crop and would love to know how you created the espalier thingummyjig please!
@curatoromiscellany
Ah, the espalier thingummyjig, otherwise known as *'that fancy apple tree that looks like it's been to pilates'*. It's actually simpler than it looks!

I started with a young, flexible apple tree and trained the main stems horizontally along strong wires, which were fixed to posts or a wall at 45cm intervals. Each spring, I tie in new side shoots to keep those tiers neat and symmetrical, and snip off any rebels trying to grow the wrong way.

The trick is patience and structure. Think of it as garden origami. Once the tree is trained, it stays in shape beautifully and produces loads of fruit without taking up much space.

How do you know which plants can be propagated and how do you know which ones to put in water or dirt?
@jeeezzkaan
Here's the truth: most garden plants can be propagated, but *how* you do it depends on the type of plant.

- **Soft, green-stemmed plants** (like mint, basil or coleus) are the easy ones, as they'll often root in water or damp compost. They're quick, forgiving and perfect for beginners.
- **Woody or shrubby plants** (like lavender, rosemary, hydrangea or fuchsia) prefer to root straight into soil or compost. Their thicker stems need that close contact with moisture and warmth to send out roots.

If you're not sure which way to go, here's my go-to tip: try both. Pop one cutting in water and one in compost and see which takes first. You'll soon start to notice patterns. It's one of those things you learn best by experimenting.

It's been my first year gardening and I've absolutely loved my summer flowers grown from seed. However, I'm feeling really disheartened as we enter winter. No more mooching around doing odd jobs and unfortunately most of my flowers have passed. How can we extend the colours throughout winter? What's your advice on winter flowers? And gardens over winter?
@emmamitchell93

I'll try my best to explain this briefly, but honestly, this question's big enough for its own chapter. Winter can feel like a bit of a comedown after summer – no more pottering around in shorts, no more flowers bursting everywhere. But your garden's not dead; it's just resting.

If you want colour, go for hardy winter stars like hellebores, pansies, violas and heathers – they'll keep things cheerful when everything else looks fed up. Add a few evergreens or colourful dogwood stems, and you've got structure and life through the cold months.

Here's the secret: winter's not the end of gardening, it's the prep season. Plan, tidy, mulch and just enjoy how peaceful it all feels. Once those first snowdrops appear, you'll be itching to get going again, I promise.

Please can you cover how to do a successful bulb lasagne/trifle? I'm really confused about planting depths. And how can I stop pesky squirrels digging up my bulbs?
@cappersally

Bulb lasagnes sound fancy, but they're basically just layers of bulbs in one pot so they flower one after another.

Get a deep pot with drainage holes. Big bulbs (like tulips) go at the bottom, middle-sized ones (hyacinths, narcissi) in the middle and small ones (crocus, muscari) on top. Always cover each layer with compost before adding the next.

Now, about those squirrels – they're absolute menaces. You can stop them by laying a bit of chicken wire just under the surface of the soil, or sprinkle dried chilli flakes over the top.

I cannot grow hydrangeas! I love them, but they all die. Please send help! Or at least advice. Yours are lovely.
@cakeali

Ah, the hydrangea heartbreak – you're not alone! They look tough but can be surprisingly fussy.

Here's the quick fix: shade, moisture and mulch. They hate drying out, so keep the soil consistently damp (not soggy), and mulch around the base to lock in water. Morning sun and afternoon shade is perfect. Full sun cooks them; deep shade sulks them.

And as for pruning, I go into full detail on when and how to prune them properly in the pruning chapter (see pages 186–7), so definitely check that before you reach for the secateurs!

Get those three right, and you'll finally have hydrangeas showing off instead of giving up.

YOUR BIGGEST GARDENING QUESTIONS – ANSWERED!

Our roses keep dying. Some people say, 'don't let water from the hose get on the flower and stem.' Why? Are we cutting them back at the wrong time (autumn/fall)? Should they get fertiliser every spring? What really works to keep them healthy and thriving every year? It's so frustrating.
@teatimemd

Roses can be dramatic and gorgeous, but also full of attitude. The good news is, once you understand what they like, they're actually pretty easy.

First off, yes, avoid constantly soaking the leaves and blooms when watering. It's not fatal, but it can encourage fungal problems like black spot or mildew. Water straight to the roots instead.

As for pruning, autumn is too early. You'll find the full lowdown in my pruning chapter (page 175), but in short: tidy lightly in autumn if they're messy, then do your main prune in late winter or early spring when the buds start to swell.

And yes, a spring feed works wonders. Use a balanced fertiliser or rose feed just as they start growing. Add a good mulch after feeding to lock in moisture and protect the roots.

How do you successfully move MASSIVE shrubs that have been planted in the most inconvenient places? I don't want to keep wrestling with a rose bush every time I need to get in or out of the car!
@carys.92

Moving big shrubs (especially roses) can be done, but it's all about timing and prep.

The best time is late autumn to early spring, when the plant is dormant. Water it well a day before you move it, then dig a wide circle around the base to capture as much of the root ball as possible. Don't go for depth – first go wide, then under.

Once it's free, replant it straight away at the same depth it was before, in a hole that's wider than the root ball. Water deeply, mulch well and resist the urge to prune too hard immediately. Let it settle in.

If it's really huge, cut it back a bit before digging to make it manageable and reduce stress on the roots. Roses will forgive you as long as they're kept watered for the first few months.

What plants are best to encourage birds into the garden?
@lindaoriordan

If you want more birds in your garden, think berries, seeds and shelter. Go for hawthorn, holly, ivy and rowan for berries and nesting spots, and sunflowers or teasels for seed heads they can feast on. Even a small native hedge gives them food and cover.

And don't tidy too much! Leaving seed heads and a few scruffy corners in winter is the best invitation you can offer.

Should I bring my herb plants inside for the winter and will they actually survive inside? Do I have to change care when inside? I can't seem to keep my rosemary, basil and thyme plants for more than one summer season.
@cproctor221
That's a really common problem – herbs can be fussy in winter!

Basil hates the cold, so yes, bring it indoors before frost. Keep it on a bright windowsill, water lightly and don't let it sit in soggy soil. Even then, it's short-lived and most people just re-sow basil each spring.

Thyme and rosemary are tougher. They're Mediterranean herbs, so they prefer cool, dry conditions and plenty of light. If your winters are mild and soil drains well, they can stay outside. But if your garden's wet or frosty, move pots to a sheltered, sunny spot or an unheated greenhouse. Indoors, they'll need as much light as possible and be careful with watering, as too much water usually kills them.

In short: basil's a house guest, and rosemary and thyme can tough it out if they're kept dry and bright!

I'm in a rented property. The original tenants built a raised bed at the bottom of the garden, but it gets almost zero sunlight. What are the best plants/flowers to plant in an area like this?
@polingchromes
Ah, the classic 'shady raised bed at the bottom of the garden' problem. Lots of people seem to inherit one!

If it's full shade most of the day, go for plants that actually *enjoy* it rather than fight it. Think ferns, hostas, heucheras, foxgloves, pulmonaria and astilbes. They thrive in low light and still look great. Add some ivy or brunnera ('Jack Frost') for year-round texture.

If you fancy flowers, begonias and impatiens (busy Lizzies) give great colour even in shade.

Just make sure the soil stays moist but not soggy. Shady gardens dry out more slowly, but still need consistent water. And if it's deep, dark shade under trees, maybe lean into it and add bark, ferns and moss to turn it into a calm, woodland-style corner.

What would your recommendation be to prevent leatherjackets, which seem to be incredibly common in new-build gardens?
@carlysamantha
Leatherjackets are the larvae of crane flies (those big, gangly daddy long-legs that dive-bomb you in September). They love new-build lawns because the soil is compacted, damp and full of fresh turf roots to munch on.

The trick is to break the cycle early:
- **Aerate** your lawn in autumn and spring. Leatherjackets hate dry, well-drained soil.
- **Rake out thatch** so they've got nowhere cosy to hide.
- If you've had a real infestation, **use nematodes** (biological control) in late summer or early autumn when the larvae are small – it's a natural, pet-safe fix.

Avoid overwatering and compacting the lawn and keep it healthy with regular feeding. A strong lawn can shrug off most pests.

YOUR BIGGEST GARDENING QUESTIONS – ANSWERED!

When should I cut my lavender back, and by how much?
@following.petula.joy

Lavender's one of those plants people either trim too hard or not enough. In the UK, the best time to prune is late summer, just after it's finished flowering (usually August or early September).

Here's the trick:
- Cut back the spent flower stalks and about one-third of the soft green growth but never into the old woody stems, or it might not regrow.
- Shape it into a neat dome to stop it going leggy or splitting open over winter.

In spring, just give it a light tidy to remove any winter damage. Keep that balance and your lavender will stay compact, bushy and full of flowers for years.

Lily beetles – how do I manage these without pesticides? I've tried neem oil but still getting eggs and then the cycle starts all over. I've resorted to hand-picking them with gloves, putting them in a ziplock and throwing in the garbage, but I'm losing and each year we get more. I'm assuming they burrow into the soil and come back every spring?
@mrsmarryat

Look cute – absolute menace. You're right, they overwinter in the soil, so they keep coming back for round two (and three). You're doing the right thing hand-picking them – it's gross, but effective.

Here are a few other tricks:
- Check daily in spring, especially under leaves, and squash or wipe off any red eggs.
- Watch for grubs covered in their own poo (disgusting but true). Wash or wipe them off.
- Blast with water to knock them off before they lay more eggs.
- Replace the top few inches of soil in spring to remove overwintering beetles.
- Add a bit of grit mulch – it makes egg-laying harder.

Consistency's the key. Keep at it, and you'll start breaking the cycle. We've all had that 'talking to beetles on our knees' moment, it's a gardener's rite of passage.

What plant could you not live without?
@mossandfeathercreative

That's such a tough one. But if I had to choose, it would be a fern. There's just something timeless about them. They're ancient, elegant and somehow make any corner of the garden feel calm.

Ferns don't scream for attention with big flowers or bright colours; they just exist quietly, softening everything around them. I love how they unfurl in spring – those little curled fronds slowly opening like nature stretching after a long nap. They thrive in the shadier spots where other plants sulk, filling them with texture and life.

For me, ferns are like the heartbeat of the garden – constant, grounding and full of quiet resilience. You can neglect them a bit, move them about, forget to fuss, and they still bring that lush, ancient green magic.

My garden is thoroughly waterlogged in the winter but as dry as the Sahara in the summer. What can I plant that will enjoy both of these extreme conditions, or should I just stick with pots and tubs?
@rachelf1310

Ah, the classic British garden – flooded in winter, desert in summer! It's a tricky combo, but not impossible. The key is to improve your soil with compost or well-rotted manure so it drains better in winter and holds moisture in summer.

If you still want to plant in the ground, go for tough, adaptable choices like:
- **Siberian iris** – loves wet feet in winter but handles summer dryness.
- **Astilbe** – thrives in damp but copes when things dry out.
- **Daylilies** – near indestructible and happy in both extremes.
- **Cornus (dogwood)** – brilliant colour and doesn't mind soggy soil.

If your soil's truly unpredictable, pots might be your best friend. You control the drainage, the feed and where they live. Sometimes the smartest gardening is knowing when to bring the plants up rather than keep fighting the ground.

Is it safe to use dry leaves as mulch? If so, do they need to be shredded or left to rot first?
@aimee_monty85

Absolutely, dry leaves make fantastic mulch, and they're totally safe to use. In fact, they're one of the best freebies your garden gives you.

If you've got time, shredding them first (with a mower or trimmer) helps them break down faster and stops them forming a soggy mat that blocks air and water. But if that sounds like too much effort, you can still use them whole, just spread them in a light layer around plants and not too thickly.

Alternatively, bag them up in autumn, poke a few holes in the bags and let them rot down over winter. By spring or next autumn, you'll have beautiful, crumbly leaf mould, which is one of the best soil conditioners going.

So yes, use those leaves! Whether shredded, whole, or half-rotted, they'll feed your soil, keep moisture in and protect roots from frost – all for free.

How do I manage my compost bin? I put stuff in there, but what am I meant to do then?
@woodsestelle

Brilliant question and, honestly, one that loads of people secretly wonder about! Most of us start a compost bin with great intentions, then stare at it months later thinking, 'Right... now what?'

Once you've started adding your kitchen and garden waste, the trick is balance and movement. Compost needs a mix of:
- **Greens** – things that rot fast and are full of moisture (veg peelings, grass cuttings, coffee grounds).
- **Browns** – drier stuff that adds structure (cardboard, twigs, dried leaves, paper).

Aim for roughly a 50/50 mix. Too many greens and it goes slimy and smelly. Too many browns and it dries out and stalls.

Every few weeks, give it a turn or mix with a fork – this adds air, which speeds everything up. If it looks dry, sprinkle a bit of water; if it looks like soup, add more cardboard.

Then... leave it alone. Composting takes time. You'll know it's ready when it's dark, crumbly and smells earthy, not rotten.

Composting is a bit like cooking a slow stew – mix it right, stir occasionally and let time do the rest. I cover this in more detail on page 59.

I don't have a garden, but I do have a south-facing balcony with lots of sun. Which plants thrive there?
@andrearaaijmakers1983
A sunny, south-facing balcony is a dream – it's basically a mini Mediterranean garden waiting to happen. The key is to pick plants that love the heat, don't mind a bit of drying out and can handle pots.

For summer colour, go for:
- **Lavender** – loves full sun and gives you scent, colour and pollinators galore.
- **Geraniums** – thrive in heat and bloom for months.
- **Thyme, rosemary and oregano** – herbs that double up as beautiful foliage plants.
- **Zinnias or cosmos** – great annuals that add bold colour and height.

Yes, you can absolutely turn your balcony into a little paradise. Just think 'sun-lovers in summer, tough cookies in winter', and you'll have colour all year round.

Help! I have clay soil, what plants will work best?
@manxjellybean
Clay soil can feel like the enemy at first – sticky when wet, cracked when dry – but honestly, once you get to know it, it's secretly brilliant. It's rich in nutrients and holds moisture well, which means plants don't go thirsty in summer. You just need to choose ones that can handle its heavy texture. I have clay soil too.

Some of the best clay-loving plants include:
- **Roses** – they thrive in that moisture-retaining soil.
- **Hostas** – perfect if you've got a bit of shade.
- **Hydrangeas** – they adore clay and reward you with masses of blooms.
- **Rudbeckia and echinacea** – bold summer flowers that don't mind a heavier soil.
- **Daylilies (hemerocallis)** – practically bulletproof and love moisture.
- **Willow and cornus (dogwood)** – great shrubs or small trees for wetter patches.

To make clay easier to work with, mix in compost, leaf mould or well-rotted manure every year – it improves drainage and stops it turning to concrete in summer.

Can you please help with the most controversial peony question: 'to prune or not to prune?' When is best for the different varieties and how far down do you cut? I trust ya Johnny!
@mama_arnold96
To prune or not to prune! The answer depends entirely on which type you've got.

Herbaceous peonies (the most common kind) die back each year. Once the leaves turn yellow and flop in autumn, cut them right down to 5–8cm above the soil. It keeps things tidy and prevents diseases like peony wilt.

Tree peonies are woody shrubs. Don't cut them back hard or you'll lose next year's blooms. Just snip off any dead or damaged stems in late winter and leave the framework intact.

Quick check: if the base is soft and green, it's herbaceous; if it's woody and branched, it's a tree peony.

Prune the soft ones, leave the woody ones and you'll have jaw-dropping blooms every year.

How do I get rid of bamboo or at least keep it under control? We moved into a new home with a garden full of bamboo. It grows everywhere!
Julia KH

This is like the garden version of a horror film. Lovely to look at... until it starts popping up in your lawn, borders and next door's drive.

First, you need to know what you're dealing with:

- **Clumping bamboo** grows in tight clumps and is easier to manage.
- **Running bamboo** (the real troublemaker) sends out underground runners that spread like wildfire.

If it's running bamboo, here's how to fight back:

1. **Dig and divide:** Start by digging out as much as you can. You'll need to chase those rhizomes (underground stems), as they can run metres away from the original plant.
2. **Barrier method:** If you want to keep some, dig a trench around it and line it with root barrier membrane or thick paving slabs, about 60cm deep, to stop it spreading.
3. **Regular maintenance:** Mow or cut any new shoots as soon as they appear outside the barrier. Starving the plant of energy will slowly weaken it.
4. **Contain in pots:** If you still want the look, grow bamboo in large containers – it looks great but can't escape.

Bamboo's persistence is impressive, but with a bit of determination (and possibly some swearing), you *can* win. Just remember, never underestimate its ability to sneak back when you're not looking!

After blooming marvellously all summer, how should I care for my dalia tubers through the winter months?
Hannah Woods (this.bird.inked)

Ah, dahlias – absolute show-offs in summer, but total divas in winter. Once the first frost hits and the foliage turns black, that's your signal to step in.

I've tried both methods over the years: lifting and storing versus leaving them in the ground. Honestly, I'm going back to leaving them put and mulching heavily. It just saves time and the results have been great.

Here's what to do either way:

- Cut back the stems to about 10–15cm once the frost hits.
- If your soil is free-draining and you're not in a frost pocket, pile on a thick mulch (compost, straw or bark) to insulate the tubers.

- If you're somewhere colder or waterlogged, lift them carefully, dry them for a week and store them in compost or sawdust in a frost-free spot.

For me, mulching wins – less faff, less chance of them shrivelling in storage and they bounce back strong in spring. Sometimes the simplest way really is the best.

Does it make a difference what type of soil you use for different types of plants?
Kelly Forde

Oh absolutely, soil makes *all* the difference. You can have the prettiest pots and the best plants, but if the soil's not right, you're basically asking them to live in the wrong postcode.

There are a few key things to think about:

1. pH

This is how acidic or alkaline your soil is. It's measured on a scale from 1 to 14, with 7 being neutral.
- **Acidic soil (below 7)** suits plants like rhododendrons, azaleas, camellias and heathers.
- **Alkaline soil (above 7)** is great for plants like lavender, lilac and clematis.

If you're not sure, do a quick pH test (you can buy kits online or in garden centres). Once you know, you can choose plants that love what you've already got – much easier than trying to change it.

2. Drainage.

Plants hate having 'wet feet'. Soggy soil suffocates roots and leads to rot. If your garden is heavy clay and holds water, dig in compost or grit to improve drainage. On the other hand, if your soil's super-sandy and water runs straight through, add organic matter like compost or leaf mould to help it hold moisture.

3. Texture and structure.

You'll hear gardeners talk about **clay**, **loam** and **sand**.
- **Clay** is rich but sticky and slow-draining.
- **Sand** is light and dry.
- **Loam** is the dream – a perfect mix of both, holding water but draining well too.

Adding organic matter regularly (compost, manure, leaf mould) helps every soil type behave better.

4. Food and life.

Healthy soil isn't just 'dirt'. It's full of worms, microbes and fungi working behind the scenes to feed your plants. The more organic matter you add, the happier this underground community is and the better your plants will grow.

In short: soil is everything. Know what you've got, work with it and feed it well – and your plants will thank you by thriving. I always say gardening isn't just about growing plants; it's about growing good soil first.

How do I get rid of bindweed? You can't say blow up your garden!
Alisha Burrell

Bindweed, the plant equivalent of that one guest who turns up uninvited, eats all the snacks and refuses to leave. And no, sadly, I can't tell you to blow up your garden.

Here's the honest truth, you'll never get rid of bindweed overnight, but you *can* beat it with patience and persistence.

1. **Dig, don't chop.**
   The roots snap easily, and each tiny bit left behind grows into a new plant – it's basically the Hydra of the garden world. Use a fork (not a spade) and tease out as much root as you can, following those white spaghetti-like strands deep into the soil.
2. **Starve it.**
   If you can't dig it all out, *deny it light*. Cover the area with thick cardboard or black plastic for a season. No light = no photosynthesis = eventually, no bindweed.
3. **Twirl and isolate.**
   If it's growing through your borders, train the shoots up a cane or stick rather than letting them smother your plants. That way, you can spot and remove it easily without ripping up half your bed.
4. **Avoid composting it.**
   Bindweed laughs in the face of compost bins – it'll survive and spread. Bin it instead.

I won't lie, it's one of the toughest weeds out there. But stick with it. A mix of digging, starving and sheer stubbornness will win in the end. And when you do finally see that patch free of white twirls, it'll feel so satisfying.

Please tell me how to get rid of clover in my beautiful lawn?
Elly Hofman

The Marmite of the grass world. Some gardeners love it (the bees certainly do), but I get it – if you've spent hours chasing perfect stripes, those little white dots can drive you mad.

Here's the good news: clover only takes over when the grass is struggling, so it's more of a symptom than a villain. The secret is strengthening your lawn, so the clover doesn't stand a chance.

Here's what to do:
1. **Feed your lawn.**
   Clover thrives in poor soil because it can make its own nitrogen. Give your grass a balanced feed (spring and autumn) and it'll outcompete the clover naturally.
2. **Raise your mower height.**
   Longer grass shades the clover and helps the lawn thicken up. Scalping the lawn only encourages it.
3. **Regular scarifying and overseeding.**
   In autumn, rake out thatch and moss, then overseed. Fresh grass seed fills any gaps where clover likes to sneak in.
4. **Weed by hand (if it's not everywhere).**
   For small patches, a lawn weeder works brilliantly – twist and pull out the whole root.
5. **Stay consistent.**
   Clover loves neglect. If you keep feeding, mowing properly and overseeding once a year, you'll see it fade back naturally.

Personally? I've come to tolerate a *tiny* bit of clover, as it keeps the bees happy and the lawn green through summer droughts. But if you're after that crisp, stripe-perfect look, regular care and a well-fed lawn will always be your best weapon.

Fern trees: *Dicksonia antarctica*. When is the best time to wrap it? And should you leave the ferns?
Cookes Wild Ride

Dicksonia antarctica looks like something straight out of *Jurassic Park*, but sadly doesn't enjoy our British winters.

When to wrap:
Start thinking about protection once night temperatures drop consistently below 5°C, usually around late October to early November in most parts of the UK. Don't rush to wrap too early though; you want to let the crown breathe for as long as possible before you tuck it in for its winter nap.

How to wrap:
- The most important part to protect is the crown (that fuzzy, fibre-filled bit where the new fronds emerge).
- Stuff the crown gently with dry straw, fleece or scrunched newspaper, then cover the top with a layer of horticultural fleece or even an upturned plant pot to keep out the rain.
- If it's a particularly harsh winter where you are, you can also wrap the trunk with fleece or hessian to stop it freezing solid.

Leave or cut the fronds?
If they're still green and healthy, leave them on. They give the crown a bit of extra insulation and help protect it from frost. Once they turn brown and collapse, you can cut them off in spring when you see new growth unfurling.

In short: wrap late autumn, unwrap in spring and let it hibernate in style.

How do you avoid seasonal depression when you see all your hard work from spring and summer just dying off? I know it will come back next year, but it really does depress me to see it.
Peter Jones

I get this one a lot and, I'll be honest, I feel it too. You spend months nurturing every leaf, petal and blade of grass, then suddenly it's all turning brown and slumping over like it's had enough of life. It can feel a bit like saying goodbye to an old friend.

But here's the thing: nothing in the garden is really dying, it's just resting. What looks like an ending is actually a pause, a deep breath before next year's burst of life. Nature needs that downtime. To be honest, so do we.

I try to flip my mindset: instead of mourning what's fading, I start planning what's next. Autumn and winter are my reset seasons, the time to dream up new ideas, sketch plans, clean tools and just be in the garden without rushing. There's something really grounding about that slower pace.

If you struggle with the darker days, bring the green indoors. A few houseplants, a pot of bulbs on the windowsill, even some cut stems from the garden, it's amazing how a bit of living colour and a plant or two to tend can lift your mood.

So yes, it's hard watching the garden fade, but it's also the universe's way of reminding us to slow down, recharge and grow again come spring.

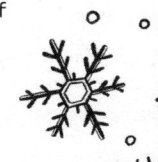

What are the best shrubs or small trees for a small garden that offer year-round interest and won't grow too large?
@De8s

This is the holy grail of small gardens. Plants that look good all year, don't turn into monsters and still give you something to show off about when the neighbours peek over the fence.

The trick is to pick compact, slow-growing varieties that give you a bit of everything: evergreen structure, seasonal flowers, berries, scent or interesting bark. Think of them as your garden's all-weather performers – the ones who don't clock off when summer ends.

Here are some of my favourites:
- *Skimmia japonica* – Evergreen, neat and tidy, with shiny leaves and red berries in winter. Brilliant for shady corners and stays small.
- *Daphne odora* – Compact and evergreen with incredibly fragrant pink flowers in late winter and early spring. You'll smell it before you see it.
- *Osmanthus delavayi* – A hidden gem with glossy leaves and sweet-scented white blooms in spring. Great shape and behaves itself.
- *Choisya ternata* (Mexican orange blossom) – Evergreen with citrusy leaves and starry white flowers that pop twice a year if it's happy.
- *Acer palmatum* (Japanese maple) – Not evergreen but makes up for it with stunning spring foliage and fiery autumn colour. Perfect for pots or partial shade.

When space is tight, one or two well-chosen shrubs can give your garden structure through winter and personality through the seasons. Pair an evergreen backbone (like Skimmia or Osmanthus) with something that flowers or changes colour, and you'll have year-round interest without ever needing a chainsaw.

Small garden, big impact – that's the goal.

Why has my wisteria not flowered yet? It's six years in. When do I cut it back? How hard do I go?
@vikkiharrismerrick

Wisteria is beautiful, dramatic and stubborn as anything. If yours hasn't flowered after six years, don't give up. Some take up to ten years to mature, especially if grown from seed rather than grafted (look for a little join near the base if it's grafted).

Common reasons for no blooms:
- **Too much nitrogen** – all leaf, no flower.
- **Not enough sun** – it needs a bright, sunny wall.
- **No pruning routine** – this one's key.

Here's the simple fix:
- **Summer (July–Aug)**: shorten new whippy shoots to five or six leaves.
- **Winter (Jan–Feb)**: cut those same shoots again to two or three buds from the main stem.

This controls growth and encourages flower buds instead of endless greenery.

So ease off the feed, give it sun and prune it twice a year. Once it's ready, it'll reward you with a floral show that is worth the wait.

Thank you so much for the questions! I honestly enjoyed answering them all.

And there we have it – proof that no matter how many gardening books, experts or fancy Latin names you come across, the best questions always come straight from real gardeners. From ferns to fruit trees, from stubborn wisteria to the winter blues, these are the thoughts that keep us all grounded (literally).

The thing I love most about answering your questions is that they remind me that we're all learning together. Gardening isn't about knowing everything; it's about curiosity, patience and sometimes admitting you've got no idea why your peony's giving you attitude this year.

Every garden tells a story, and every question adds a new page to it. So, keep asking, keep experimenting and don't worry if your dahlias flop or your lawn looks like it's been through a festival – it's all part of the journey.

13
GARDENING MYTHS
Separating the Weeds from the Wisdom

Every gardener has *that* friend or neighbour. You know the one – the person who swears that sprinkling coffee grounds makes hydrangeas turn blue, that banana skins will make your roses 'burst with joy' and that if you plant by the light of the full moon, your carrots will grow straighter. Bless them.

The truth is, gardening might be full of joy, but it's also full of myths. Some harmless, some hilarious and some that cause more damage than slugs at midnight. We've all fallen for a few. I certainly have. I once tried watering my plants with leftover tea because someone told me it was 'natural plant food'. All I managed to do was make the border smell like a canteen and attract ants. Lesson learned.

The trouble is, gardening advice gets passed down like folklore. Someone's granddad swore by it, their neighbour copied it and before you know it, it's written in stone. These days, you only need to scroll a few posts online to find someone confidently sprinkling kitchen cupboard ingredients over their plants and calling it a 'miracle hack'. Spoiler: most of those miracles end in wilted leaves and regret.

But here's the thing: not every old wives' tale is wrong. Some of those weird bits of advice actually work. There's often a nugget of truth buried under the nonsense. The trick is knowing which ones to keep and which ones to politely bin (or compost).

In this chapter, we're going to bust some of the biggest gardening myths. The ones whispered down through generations, the ones plastered across TikTok and those muttered by well-meaning neighbours everywhere. I'll tell you which ones are rubbish, which ones are surprisingly true and which ones fall somewhere in that murky middle ground of 'it depends'.

We'll cover everything from the myths that kill plants faster than neglect, to the ones that genuinely make your soil and garden better. I'll even share a few of my own 'I can't believe I tried that' moments, because – believe me – I've fallen for a fair few of these myself.

Before we get into it, a little disclaimer: gardening isn't an exact science. Sometimes a myth works for one gardener because of their soil, climate or sheer luck, then it fails miserably for someone else. That's what keeps it interesting. The garden's always got a mind of its own.

So, grab a brew (or a banana skin, if you must), and let's separate the green-fingered facts from the flowery fiction. Because while the internet might love a quick hack, you and your plants deserve the truth.

Myths

Myth: 'You Must Dig or Rotavate Your Soil Every Year.'
(Turns out the best soil care is often the laziest)

For decades, gardeners were told to dig their soil every winter. Turn it over, break it up, 'let the frost in'. It looks productive, sure, but in reality all that effort does more harm than good.

Soil isn't just dirt. It's a living ecosystem packed with worms, fungi and microbes quietly doing all the hard work for you. When you dig or rotavate, you tear apart that network, breaking up the natural structure and exposing those organisms to frost and sun. It's a bit like walking into a perfectly organised kitchen and mixing all the drawers together for fun.

That's where **no-dig gardening** comes in. Instead of turning everything over, you simply feed the surface. Add a layer of compost or well-rotted manure each year and let the worms do the mixing. They'll pull it down naturally, improving drainage and structure, while you sit back and admire your efficiency.

The moment I stopped and trusted the worms, my beds stayed softer, moister and easier to manage.

Myth: 'You Should Water Every Day.'

(Spoiler: You're drowning them, not loving them)

This one's a classic and I talked about this in an earlier chapter (see pages 69–70). So many new gardeners think that watering every day shows dedication. The more water, the happier the plants, right? Sadly, that's how you end up with soggy soil, weak roots and limp, miserable plants that keel over the second you skip a day.

Here's the truth: watering little and often just keeps moisture near the surface. The roots stay shallow because they never need to reach deeper down. Then a hot day arrives, and suddenly everything wilts. You've basically trained your plants to be lazy and dependent.

Instead, **water deeply but less often.** Give the soil a proper soak, then leave it to dry slightly before watering again. This encourages roots to grow deep and strong, where they can find their own moisture.

There are a couple of exceptions, like pots and hanging baskets. Because they dry out quicker and don't have access to deeper soil, they'll need checking more often, especially in summer. Even then, check before you water. If the top 2–3cm of compost feels dry, go for it; if it's still damp, leave it be.

So, next time you feel the urge to grab the hose every evening, resist. Step back, have a brew and let your plants learn a bit of independence.

Myth: 'The More Fertiliser, The Better.'
(Otherwise known as: How to accidentally deep-fry your plants)

Ah yes, the 'more must be better' logic. I fell for this one myself. I used to fling fertiliser around like Parmesan on pasta (yum), thinking I'd have the greenest, lushest plants in the street. Instead, I ended up with yellow patches, crispy leaves and roots that looked like they'd been microwaved.

Here's the thing: fertiliser is powerful stuff. Plants need nutrients like nitrogen for leafy growth, phosphorus for roots and potassium for strength, but only in balance. When you dump on too much, salts build up in the soil and draw moisture out of the roots. The result? Burned roots, stunted growth and a plant that looks like it's just had a rough night out.

Most gardens don't actually need feeding as often as people think. **A couple of well-timed feeds a year is plenty**. And if you use compost, mulch or organic matter, that's feeding the soil naturally anyway.

So, instead of thinking of fertiliser like a magic potion, treat it more like seasoning. A pinch adds flavour, a bucket ruins dinner.

Myth: 'You Must Prune Everything in Winter.'
(Spoiler: Spring bloomers will hate you for it)

This one catches loads of people out, especially when the gardening books and TV shows start shouting 'winter pruning season!' The problem? Not every plant wants a haircut when it's freezing. In fact, if you prune the wrong thing in winter, you're basically chopping off next year's flowers before they've even had a chance. I've dedicated a whole chapter to pruning (see page 175), so make sure you go back and take a look if you're unsure what to prune when!

Here's the golden rule: **if it flowers in spring, don't prune it in winter**. Plants like forsythia, lilac and camellia form their flower buds the previous summer. So, if you come along with the secateurs in January, snipping away like Edward Scissorhands, you're cutting

off the very stems that would have bloomed. Cue a sad, flowerless spring. Instead, prune these right after they finish flowering. That way, they've got the rest of the year to regrow and form new buds for next season.

Winter pruning is perfect for plants that bloom later in the year. Think roses, buddleia, hydrangea *paniculata* and shrubs grown for colourful stems. They flower on fresh growth, so pruning in winter encourages strong new shoots come spring.

Before you pick up the secateurs, take a second to check when your plant actually flowers. If it's a spring bloomer, step away slowly. If it's a summer or autumn one, grab those secateurs with confidence.

Myth: 'Cutting Grass Really Short Keeps it Neat Longer.'
(Actually, you're just giving it a stress haircut)

Ah, the temptation. You drag the mower out, drop the blades to the lowest setting and think, *'Right, I'll scalp it once and won't need to mow for ages.'* For a day or two, it looks tidy. Then the sun comes out and your 'neat' lawn turns the colour of Weetabix.

Here's the truth: **mowing too short weakens the grass**. Each blade of grass is basically a little solar panel. Chop it too low, and the plant can't photosynthesise properly. That means it can't make enough energy to grow or repair itself, so it turns pale, patchy and weak. And when grass is weak, weeds move in like uninvited guests at a barbecue.

The golden rule? Never cut off more than one-third of the grass height at a time. If your lawn is 9cm tall, don't mow lower than 6cm. In summer, go even higher (around 5-7cm). Longer blades shade the soil, keep moisture in and make the lawn far more resilient to heat and drought.

Myth: 'Eggshells Stop Slugs.'
(Sorry – your breakfast isn't a forcefield)

This one refuses to die. You'll see it all over gardening groups: *Just scatter crushed eggshells around your plants, slugs won't dare cross!* I hate to break it to you, but slugs are tougher (and slimier) than that. They'll glide right over your eggshell barrier without a care in the world. I've watched them do it in my own garden. It's like an obstacle course made of snacks.

The theory sounds good, sharp edges deterring soft bellies, but in practice the shells break down too quickly, and the edges blunt almost immediately once they get damp. Add a bit of rain, and your once-spiky 'defence line' turns into harmless garden confetti.

Now, that's not to say eggshells are useless. They're actually decent for adding calcium to your compost or working into the soil when you're planting tomatoes and peppers (both of which love a bit of calcium). But as a slug deterrent? Total myth.

If you really want to keep slugs off your plants, go for methods that work:
- **Wool pellets** or **copper tape** around pots. They actually bother the slugs enough to turn back.
- **Beer traps** – old-school but effective (apparently, slugs love lager).
- Encourage **natural predators** like frogs, hedgehogs and birds – they're your best long-term defence.

Save the eggshells for compost. When it comes to slug control, you'll need something a little more serious than breakfast leftovers.

Myth: 'Coffee Grounds Are an All-Purpose Fertiliser.'
(Spoiler: Not every plant likes a latte)

Coffee grounds have had quite the glow-up in recent years from kitchen waste to 'miracle fertiliser' according to half of the internet. The idea is tempting: sprinkle your morning leftovers on the soil and boom – instant plant food. Sadly, it's not quite that simple.

While coffee grounds do contain small amounts of nutrients like nitrogen, potassium and magnesium, they're not a balanced fertiliser, and they can actually cause more harm than good if you use too much. Fresh grounds are quite acidic, which means they can mess with your soil's pH, and not all plants appreciate that. Acid-loving plants like blueberries, azaleas, camellias and hydrangeas (the blue ones) might enjoy the occasional sprinkle, but for most others it's a bit like giving them ten espressos and wondering why they're looking twitchy.

On top of that, coffee grounds can form a crust on the surface of the soil, which actually stops water from soaking through properly. So, instead of feeding your plants, you're basically waterproofing them. Not ideal.

If you really want to make use of your coffee waste, the best way is to **compost it**. Mix it with brown materials, such as cardboard or dry leaves, and it'll break down beautifully. Once it's fully composted, it's safe for all plants and gives your soil a nice boost of organic matter.

So yes, coffee grounds can be useful... just not sprinkled raw onto everything. Treat them as part of your compost, not as a miracle fertiliser. Your plants will thank you, and you can keep the caffeine for yourself.

Truths

Truth: Morning Watering Is Best
(Because plants hate a soggy bedtime)

There's a reason seasoned gardeners are out early with the hose or watering can, and that's because morning watering really is best. It's not just tradition, it's science and common sense rolled together.

When you water in the morning, the soil still holds the cool of the night, so **moisture soaks down to the roots** instead of evaporating away. The plants have all day to drink up before the heat hits, and any splashes on the leaves have time to dry off in the sun. That last bit matters more than you might think, as wet leaves overnight are an open invitation to fungal diseases like mildew and blight.

Evening watering, on the other hand, can feel lovely and peaceful… but it's also when the garden's 'night shift' (slugs, snails and fungal spores) wake up. Damp soil and dark corners make for an all-you-can-eat buffet. Morning watering gives the plants what they need and dries things up before the pests get going.

The best method? Water deeply and slowly at the base of plants, not a quick splash-and-dash. Think of it as filling a pint glass, not flicking a mist.

And, yes, I know what I look like at 7am when I'm out there watering – flip-flops on, hair all over the place, wide-legged stance like I'm performing some sort of ritual to the gardening gods. My neighbours probably think I've lost it, but my plants look fantastic, so I'll take the win.

Truth: Slow-Release Feed Is Safer for Beginners
(Because plants don't need an all-you-can-eat buffet)

When you're new to gardening, it's easy to think that more food means more growth, like plants are bodybuilders in need of constant protein shakes. But the truth is that plants prefer steady meals, not surprise banquets. That's where slow-release feeds come in – and they're an absolute lifesaver for beginners.

Slow-release fertilisers (the little pellets or coated granules you mix into the soil) break down gradually over weeks or months. Instead of dumping a load of nutrients on your plants in one go, they feed them a little at a time. Think of it as a slow cooker for your soil – consistent, gentle and no risk of burning dinner.

Liquid feeds, on the other hand, can be a bit risky if you're still finding your feet. It's easy to get the mix wrong or overdo it. Too much fertiliser can scorch roots, cause weird yellowing and make your plants sulk like you've overfed them Sunday roast and pudding.

Slow-release feed takes the guesswork out. You just scatter it at the base of plants (or mix it into compost before planting) and it quietly does its thing. Perfect for pots, borders, veg patches, pretty much anywhere.

Personally, I love it because it means I can get distracted halfway through watering or run off chasing the cat and not worry about frying my plants. If you're prone to 'enthusiastic' feeding, slow-release fertiliser is your best mate – it forgives your enthusiasm and keeps your plants happy for months.

So, if you're new to gardening and don't trust yourself with bottles and measuring caps, start slow. Literally.

Truth: Messy Gardens Help Wildlife
(Your untidy corner might just save a hedgehog's life)

If you've ever felt guilty about your 'messy' garden – the piles of leaves, the uncut grass, the dead stems you never got round to pruning – stop right there. What you call untidy, nature calls home.

Those scruffy corners and overgrown patches are absolute gold for wildlife. A heap of twigs and leaves isn't a sign you've given up, it's a luxury apartment block for beetles, woodlice and hedgehogs. Uncut seed heads? That's a winter buffet for birds and bees. Even that pile of rotting logs you've been meaning to tidy? Perfect shelter for frogs and insects.

We gardeners are often told that neat = good. Think razor-edged lawns, swept paths, not a leaf out of place. But wildlife doesn't care about symmetry. It needs **hiding spots, nesting material and food sources**, all the things we accidentally destroy when we 'tidy up'.

One of the easiest ways to help is to leave a bit of your garden wild on purpose. Let a patch of grass grow long, keep a log pile in a shady corner, or leave the last few stems of echinacea and sedum standing through winter. They'll look beautiful dusted with frost and feed the birds at the same time.

I used to stress about keeping everything pristine until I realised that the 'messy' bits were buzzing with life. Now I like to say that I garden *strategically untidily*. It's not neglect; it's good management with a cup of tea in hand. And I think without this we wouldn't be lucky enough to have our hedgehog Sonic roaming the garden.

So, next time someone comments that your garden looks a bit wild, just smile and tell them it's eco-friendly landscaping. The hedgehogs will back you up.

Truth: Worms Are a Gardener's Best Friend
(They're the tiny, slimy superheroes under your feet)

If there's one creature that deserves more respect in the garden, it's the humble worm. They might not look like much, just little pink noodles squirming through the soil, but they're quietly doing more work than most of us realise.

Worms are the **ultimate garden recyclers**. They munch their way through dead leaves, old roots and organic matter, turning it into nutrient-rich castings (that's the polite term for worm poo). That stuff is absolute gold for your soil, packed with goodness that plants love. Every time a worm wriggles through the ground, it's not just eating, it's aerating the soil too, creating tiny tunnels that let air, water and nutrients move freely down to the roots. In other words, worms do all the boring maintenance for free. No aerator, no fertiliser, no fancy gadgets required – just let them get on with it.

You can tell a healthy garden by how many worms you find. Dig a small hole and count. If you spot a few, you're in good shape. If your soil's dry, compacted or lifeless, you might need to give the worms a hand by adding compost, mulch or organic matter. They'll move in once there's food and moisture.

Kids, by the way, love discovering worms. Mine treat them like tiny pets (and occasionally name them things like 'Slimy Steve'). But even if you're not the worm-hugging type, just know that every one of those wiggly little things is working overtime to keep your garden alive and thriving.

Truth: Gardening Really Does Lift Your Mood
(It's cheaper than therapy, and comes with tomatoes)

If you've ever dragged yourself outside feeling grumpy, only to come back in half an hour later maybe a bit muddy but calmer and happier, that's not your imagination. Gardening genuinely boosts your mood. There's proper science behind it, but you don't need a lab coat to feel it.

Part of it is the benefit of movement – digging, watering, pottering. You're using your body, getting some fresh air and soaking up daylight (even if it's the British kind that comes with drizzle). It wakes you up and resets your head. Then there's the focus you need for a little while – you're not thinking about work, emails or bills, you're just thinking, *'Does this need deadheading?'* or *'Where did I put my trowel?'* **It's mindfulness, but with soil under your nails**.

There's also a strange magic in nurturing something. Watching a seed sprout or a plant recover after a tough patch gives you a quiet sense of achievement, a reminder that growth takes time and care, in the garden and in life.

As a firefighter, my job can be physically tough and emotionally draining. The garden's where I reset. Some days I'll go out there to calm down, other days to celebrate and sometimes just to hide from the chaos for ten minutes. And it works every single time.

Even science backs this up. Studies show that gardening reduces cortisol (your stress hormone) and increases serotonin (your happy one). But honestly, you don't need research to prove what most gardeners already know. A few minutes with your hands in the soil can change your whole day.

So, if you're ever feeling low, skip the doom-scrolling and head for the garden. Pull a few weeds, water a few pots, slap a compost bag if you have to. You'll come back in smiling, slightly dirtier, maybe, but definitely happier.

Truth: Talking to Plants Helps Them Grow
(It's not the chat, it's the attention)

We've all heard this one: *'If you talk to your plants, they'll grow better.'* It sounds like something your nan might say while whispering to her begonias. Honestly, she might be onto something... sort of.

Plants don't understand words (unless you've got a very special philodendron), but they do respond to **care and attention**. When you talk to them, you're usually spending time with them, checking their leaves, noticing dry soil, spotting pests early, or giving them a drink. That extra attention is what keeps them healthy, not the motivational speeches.

There's a small scientific twist, too: when we talk, we exhale carbon dioxide, which plants use for photosynthesis. So, technically, your breath is feeding them, but only a little bit. You'd need to spend hours nattering away to make a real difference, and at that point your neighbours might start to worry.

Here's where the myth earns its charm: people who talk to their plants often have the healthiest gardens, because they're engaged. You notice changes, you respond faster and you build a weird sort of bond. I've been known to mumble the odd 'You're looking good today, mate' at my dahlias or tell a hydrangea to pull itself together. It's less plant psychology, more gardener therapy.

And honestly? It works both ways. When you slow down enough to talk to a plant, you're not just helping it, you're helping yourself. It forces you to pause, breathe and focus on something small and alive. It's grounding (literally).

So yes, *talk to your plants*. Not because they need the gossip, but because it makes you pay attention, and paying attention is half the battle in gardening. Besides, if you ever catch yourself having a full conversation with your begonias, don't worry. You're not mad, you're just committed. And your garden will love you for it.

Question Everything (Even Me)

If there's one thing I've learned over the years, it's that gardening is full of opinions. Everyone's got a 'secret trick', a 'fool-proof method', or a 'never-fail rule'. Half of them swear by talking to plants, the other half say it's nonsense. Some people swear vinegar fixes everything; others call it garden murder in a bottle. The truth? Gardening isn't about rules carved in stone, it's about learning what works for you and your space.

Myths pop up in gardening for a reason. Sometimes they start with a grain of truth. Someone tried something once, it worked, and then the story spread like bindweed. But what works in one garden might be a disaster in another. Different soil, light and weather conditions and gardener habits all play a part. So take every 'hack' or 'miracle tip' (especially the ones that show up on social media) with a healthy pinch of compost.

I've believed my fair share of nonsense, too. I've watered too much, fertilised too hard and once killed an entire patch of grass by following what I *thought* was good advice. And you know what? That's how you learn. The garden is brilliant at teaching you lessons, sometimes gently, sometimes not so gently. But each mistake is part of the fun.

If I could leave you with one takeaway, it's this: be curious, but not gullible. Try things, test ideas and see what actually works in *your* garden. You'll discover that plants are far more forgiving than most of us give them credit for.

And if talking to your dahlias makes you happy, then do it. If leaving your borders a bit messy brings in more bees, brilliant. The best gardeners aren't the ones who follow every rule; they're the ones who stay curious, observant and a little bit rebellious.

So, next time someone swears that beer traps cure slugs, or that you have to dig every inch of soil each year, smile politely and then go find out for yourself. That's what makes gardening magic. In the end, it's not about proving myths wrong or right. It's about staying hands-on, open-minded and a little muddy in the process.

14
FROM SHED PRIDE TO SEEDS OF INFLUENCE

Lots of people ask me how I got to where I am, and while I don't know any big secret to success, I thought I'd share some of the social media lessons I've learned along the way, in case you're also interested in sharing your gardening journey online. This chapter will explain my journey and give some handy hints and tips for those of you wanting to start out or grow your following.

If you'd told me back in March 2020 that buying a shed would end up changing my life, I'd have laughed in your face. I wasn't thinking about 'building a brand' or 'becoming a gardening influencer' or any of that fancy stuff people talk about now. All I wanted was somewhere nice to keep my tools, somewhere that didn't have a leaky roof, a missing door or that faint smell of fox wee you get with the cheaper flat-pack jobs.

I decided to treat myself and I bought a shed. Not just any shed, this was a *proper* shed. One you stand in front of, hands on hips, and think: 'Yep... I've made it.' It was the sort of shed you keep tidy for a week, then immediately mess up by chucking muddy boots inside, and I loved it.

Naturally, I wanted to show it off. But there was a problem. Up until that point, any time I wanted to show someone my garden, I'd find myself scrolling endlessly through my phone, trying to find that picture I took weeks ago. By the time I found it, they'd either lost interest or just walked away. So, I had an idea, why not put all my garden photos in one place? Somewhere my friends and family could look without me needing to dig them out. A little online scrapbook. That's how it started, as a filing system for my plants, my lawn and – yes – my glorious new shed.

Instagram seemed like the obvious place. I made an account called **@gardenwithjonny**, posted my first picture (me standing next to the shed, grinning like I'd just been handed the keys to Buckingham Palace) and that was it.

No caption. No hashtag strategy. Nothing clever. Just me, my shed and a big daft smile. It got about ten likes, mostly from friends and relatives, and I was chuffed. Job done.

I had zero ambition for it to become anything more. Honestly, I couldn't have imagined in a million years what it would grow into. Back then, there was no 'plan', no 'content strategy', no 'personal brand'. I was just a weird bloke with a new shed and a phone camera. Looking back now, that's probably why people connected with it later on. There was no performance and no filter (literally and figuratively). Just me, my garden and whatever was making me happy that day. I wasn't trying to impress anyone, I was just sharing what I loved.

And to this day, I think that's one of the best lessons I've learned about social media: **Start with what you love, not what you think people want.**

STARTING OUT

Before Instagram reels were even a thing, I'd already been messing around on TikTok. Not with gardening content, mind you – more comedy, personality-driven stuff, a bit of gym content, lifestyle bits and the occasional meme that only about five people probably understood. I enjoyed it because it was silly, fast and not that serious (a bit like me!).

Meanwhile, my gardening Instagram was quietly sitting there, with the odd photo. I wasn't posting loads. I'd share a plant I was proud of or a corner of the garden that I'd tidied up, but I wouldn't call it 'consistent'. In fact, there was a stage where I barely touched it.

Then, Covid hit. Like everyone else, I suddenly had a lot of free time. No socialising, no gym for a while, just the family, the garden and way too much time on my hands.

Instagram had just launched reels, and I thought, 'Why not bring some of the humour I've been doing on TikTok over to my gardening page?' So I started mixing the two. Proper gardening tips with my slightly daft personality. And that's when something clicked.

It wasn't just that people liked my plant advice or lawn tips, they liked me. The weird faces, the sarcastic comments, the fact that I could go from explaining how to deadhead roses to making a joke about something completely random. I realised I'd stumbled into a little online corner of the world where I could be myself completely, and instead of getting blank stares like I might at a dinner party, I was finding my people and spreading a bit of humour along the way.

Other beautiful weirdos were out there – gardening nuts, plant lovers, lawn obsessives – and they got it. They laughed at my jokes, they nodded along when I ranted about slugs and they actually wanted to hear my tips.

I remember the first time a grass seed company reached out and said, 'We'd love to send you some free seed.' I nearly fell off my chair. Free. Grass. Seed. I'd basically made it. Forget red carpets – this was my Oscars moment.

From there, things started snowballing. More likes, more comments, more messages from people saying they enjoyed my videos and that I'd inspired them to try something new in their own garden. And that's when it hit me: this isn't just a gallery anymore, this is a community. I'm lucky to have such wonderful followers. My page is genuinely a place of joy and uplifting comments and I'm so thankful for that.

I'd found my audience, and they'd found me.

KEEPING IT REAL (WHY MY CONTENT WORKS)

From the very start, I promised myself one thing with my gardening content: I'm not going to pretend I'm perfect. Because I'm not. Far from it. And that's perfectly okay.

If you follow me expecting flawless borders, immaculate symmetry and a lawn that never has a rogue weed, you're going to be disappointed. My garden is like me – mostly tidy, sometimes a mess, occasionally questionable, but always trying its best.

I make mistakes, I plant things in the wrong spot, I forget to water and I break things (or the kids do!). Sometimes, I'll show the beautiful blooms, but other times I'll take you behind the shed to show you the absolute tip I keep meaning to tidy. It's not 'Instagram-perfect', it's *real life* and it's what people relate to and connect with.

When you admit you've just decapitated a perfectly healthy plant because you got carried away with the secateurs, people don't unfollow. They laugh and share their own disasters, and suddenly you're not just giving gardening tips, you're having a proper conversation and opening up a fun group discussion.

I think that's why my content feels approachable. I'm not standing in a spotless garden with a teleprompter, reading facts I

Googled the night before. I'm telling you about something I've actually done, usually in the moment, with the plant or lawn right in front of me. If I'm showing you how to deadhead something, it's because I'm actually doing it. If I'm giving you lawn care advice, it's because I've just been out there with the mower and done exactly what I'm explaining. It's real and honest.

This approach means my advice comes from my own garden, my own trials and errors, and not a stock photo. If I don't have a certain plant, I won't give tips on it. If I've never tried a method, I won't pretend I have. If I can't grow something (lupins are my enemy), I'll tell you. And I think people respect that. In gardening, honesty matters.

It's also why I keep a lot of the bloopers in. If I'm talking to camera and a bee flies straight into my face, you're going to see that. If I drop a trowel mid-sentence, I'll probably leave it in. If my wife and kids are making me giggle, you'll see that too. Because gardening isn't perfectly choreographed – it's muddy, unpredictable and occasionally hilarious (if I do say so myself).

If you're interested in starting a social media page, I'd really encourage you to be yourself. People will connect with you more. Be relatable and authentic – it's your biggest strength on social media where it can sometimes feel disingenuous.

I've had people tell me they feel like they're just having a chat with me in the garden. And that's exactly the vibe I want. No pressure to have a 'perfect' space, just encouragement to enjoy the process, the slugs, the weeds, the wobbly trellis and everything else being a gardener throws at you.

And maybe that's why people trust my advice. I'm not telling you what the textbook says will work, I'm explaining what worked for me, and what went completely wrong.

MY CONTENT CREATION PROCESS (AND HOW I MAKE TIME FOR IT)

People often ask me: 'How do you manage to post so much content when you're working full-time as a firefighter, have a family, a garden to look after AND go to the gym?' The short answer? I don't stop. The long answer? I plan like mad, I batch-create, I have a supportive family and I squeeze every ounce out of my day.

Let's start with the planning bit. I don't have some fancy spreadsheet with colour-coded boxes. I keep ideas in the Notes app on my phone. If I'm mowing the lawn and suddenly think of a funny hook for a reel, I'll stop, type it down, then get back to mowing (yes, my stripes have been known to go a bit wonky because of this).

When it comes to filming, I work around my shifts. If I'm on days at the fire station, I usually don't film. I want to be 100% focused on the job. So, on my days off, I'll do what I call 'content batching'. That's basically spending a few hours in the garden filming multiple videos in one go, and I'll film bits for reels, Stories and TikToks all in one session.

Editing happens in the evenings, usually when the kids are in bed. I'm often sat there in my gym shorts, trimming down footage and choosing the right music. (Pro tip: caption everything, people watch on silent far more than you think.)

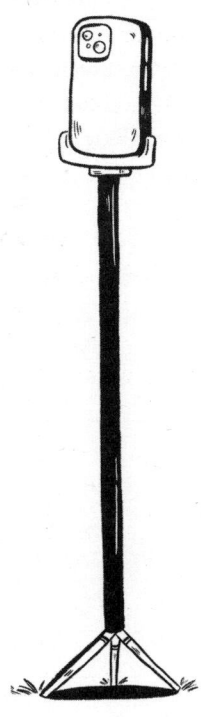

The beauty of batch-creating is that when life gets hectic – and it does – I still have videos ready to post. This keeps my account active even if I've been stuck at work or knee-deep in a big DIY project. It means I can still get content out and engage with my followers without feeling any unnecessary pressure.

There are days when I don't have anything to post, and that's fine. Going back to what I said at the start of this chapter, I never want to post anything for the sake of it – I always want any contact to be good quality, useful and engaging. Posting for the sake of posting is not something I ever want to do. Followers can sense when content is forced. Being authentic is lighter, more fun and less stressful than trying to project perfection that doesn't exist. It should always be about connection and fun, and not performance.

My Stories are different. Stories are where I'm more relaxed – no editing, no overthinking. I'll show you what I'm doing in real time, whether it's feeding the lawn, building something, or just having a cuppa (or telling some brilliant dad jokes). I don't polish my Stories – they are where I can be more off-the-cuff and chatty.

Juggling everything comes down to knowing my priorities. Family first, then work, then fitness, then gardening/content. But the truth is, they all overlap. The garden is part of my family life. Content is just me sharing what I'm already doing in the garden. The gym keeps me fit, so I can actually do the gardening without putting my back out. It all feeds into each other.

If you're reading this thinking, 'I want to create content, but I don't have time', my advice is simple:

- **Film what you're already doing.** Don't set up big fake scenarios. People love seeing real gardening.
- **Keep your phone handy.** You never know when you'll get a great shot or funny moment.
- **Batch your filming.** Trust me, it's a lifesaver when you're busy.
- **Don't stress about perfection.** If you wait for the perfect shot, you'll post nothing.

And finally, and this is perhaps the most important thing: enjoy the process. If you're not having fun making the content, people can tell. I love filming and editing my videos, and that's half the reason I keep going. It shouldn't feel like a chore.

HITTING MILESTONES AND A HUGE THANK YOU

I'll be honest, the milestones still feel surreal. I can remember my first ten likes on that shed photo like it was yesterday. Ten whole people! Most of them were probably family, but still, I was buzzing.

When I hit my first 100 followers, I thought I'd made it. Then it was 1,000, then 10,000, and before I knew it, we were talking six figures. I remember hitting my first 100k and just sitting there thinking, 'How on earth has this happened? I'm just a bloke in his garden, slapping compost bags and chatting about hydrangeas.'

Here's the thing though: none of this would have happened without you. Every single person who has liked, commented, shared or messaged me has been part of this. Whether you liked one video three years ago or if you've been here on this wild journey since day one, you've contributed to this little community we've built.

I get so many lovely messages. People telling me I've made them laugh on a bad day, given them the confidence to try growing something new, or even helped them get outside more. Honestly, that stuff hits me harder than any follower count ever could. Because that's the point of all this – connection and supporting each other.

It's easy to think of social media as just numbers, but behind every like and comment is a real person who's taken a moment out of their day to engage. That's huge. So, whether you're here for the lawn tips, the woodland border obsession, the compost bag slaps, or just because you think I'm a bit of a weirdo (you're not wrong), thank you.

I'll never take it for granted. I'm humbled every single day by how supportive this community is. The gardening world, online and offline, is full of kind, generous people who genuinely want to help each other. It's not competitive, it's collaborative. And I think that's why it works.

You've given me opportunities I never dreamed of, working with brands I admire, speaking at events, meeting some incredible people and even writing this book. And it all started with a shed photo.

So, here's to you, the followers, the commenters, the sharers and even the lurkers (I see you). Without you, @gardenwithjonny would still just be a quiet little corner of the internet where I post pictures for my mates. Now it's something much bigger, and I'm so grateful to be on this journey with you.

CONCLUSION
Stay Green, Stay Gorgeous

Sitting down to write these parting words made me realise just how much has gone into these pages. Not just information, but memories, honesty and all the moments that shaped why I do what I do. This book wasn't something I ever saw coming, and the fact that you've stayed with me right to the end is something I'll never take for granted.

I haven't written this as an expert with a perfect garden or a spotless record. I've written it as a bloke who adores his little patch of earth, who still gets excited when a new shoot appears and who has made every mistake under the sun. Every tip in here, from mowing the lawn to dealing with dahlias, compost heaps and kids with watering cans, comes straight from real life – all my early mornings, muddy boots and quiet evenings where I told myself 'just one more job.'

Gardening has never been about perfection for me. It's about progress. It's about learning something new every season and forgiving yourself when it all goes wrong, because it will. Something will die, something will get munched, the weather will throw a strop and you'll definitely forget to water something important. But gardening always gives you another chance. Another spring. Another seed. Another bit of ground waiting for its moment.

If there's one message I hope you take from this book, it's simple: your garden should look like your life. Not a magazine. Not your neighbour's. Yours. Whether it's a balcony, a sprawling plot, a messy lawn, or a few pots on a table, your space tells your story. And honestly? It's the imperfect ones that have the most soul.

When I posted that first photo of my shed, I never imagined it would lead to me writing an actual book, chatting to you through these pages. It all started with the idea of sharing what I loved, hoping it might make someone else smile or give gardening a go. I didn't expect the sense of connection, the messages, the comments, the photos of your gardens. They reminded me that there are thousands of us out there, all trying to grow something good, not just in our borders but in ourselves.

Gardening doesn't just change your garden. It changes you. It teaches patience. It gives clarity when life gets loud. It grounds you, literally. There's something about putting your hands in soil that resets your whole day. For me, it's been therapy after long shifts, a place to breathe, a steady reminder that growth never happens overnight.

Some moments stay with me:

> The first snowdrop pushing through.
> The smell of freshly cut grass.
> A robin keeping me company while I turn the compost.
> That quiet look around after a long day outside, thinking, 'Yeah.
> I did that.'

Those tiny moments – not the perfect photos or big reveals – are what hook you for life.

And whether you're reading this in a greenhouse, a kitchen, or a flat with a window box, I know you understand that feeling. That spark that turns you into someone who watches the sky for rain, who gets excited about worms, who talks to plants (don't lie – you absolutely do). You stop seeing 'dirt' and start seeing 'life'.

So, whether you dipped into this book for quick advice or read it cover to cover, I hope it made you feel like part of something, because you are. Every thriving border and every 'not-sure-what's-going-on-here' plant has a gardener behind it doing their best, learning as they go.

To everyone who's followed me online, asked questions, shared photos, or sent messages, thank you. You've helped build a community I'm proud of. What started as a couple of posts about a shed has turned into something real, something that matters, something I never expected.

If I could leave you with one final bit of advice, it's this: don't overthink it. Don't wait for the perfect weather, the perfect plan, or the perfect equipment. Just start. Plant something. Anything. A bulb, a seed, a cutting from your mate. Some of my best successes came from moments where I had no clue what I was doing. You learn by trying and that's half the joy. And when it goes wrong, laugh. Every gardener has a disaster story. A plant that refused to live. A squirrel with a personal vendetta. A compost bin that could've walked off on its own. Those moments give your garden character.

CONCLUSION

As you close this book and step back into your outdoor space, I hope you take something with you – curiosity over perfection, joy over frustration, connection over comparison. That's what keeps you growing, in the garden and in life.

Now, go get your hands dirty. Check the pots you forgot about. Give your plants a little pep talk. Sit outside for a minute and look at what you've created, even if it's small, messy, or a work in progress. It's yours. Your peace. Your therapy. Your little patch of magic.

And as always –

Stay Green, Stay Gorgeous.

ACKNOWLEDGEMENTS

Writing this book has been one of the most rewarding, surreal, and unexpectedly emotional journeys of my life. There were moments of absolute joy – those sparks of 'Yes, this is exactly what I wanted to say' – and moments where I wondered what on earth I'd signed myself up for. I've said throughout this book that gardening has a funny way of revealing things you didn't expect, and it turns out writing does the same.

As someone with dyslexia, sitting down to write a full book felt like climbing a mountain in flip-flops. Spelling and grammar have always been my personal nemeses, and if you'd told me back at school that one day I'd be writing a book for Penguin, I'd have laughed and then immediately checked whether you were okay. I've always been more comfortable with soil under my nails than a pen in my hand, but every page of this book reminded me that the things we find hardest often become the things we're proudest of.

And I'm proud of this. So proud.

To my wife, Jen, thank you for being my unofficial spell-checker, my sounding board and the calm voice that stopped me from launching my laptop at the wall more than once. I genuinely couldn't have done this without your support and patience (and your ability to spot a spelling mistake from across the room).

To Max and Lissy, my inspiration and my cheerleaders, thank you for reminding me why gardens matter, why stories matter and why it's important to show people that you can do anything you put your mind to, even with obstacles in the way. This book is as much yours as it is mine.

I want to give a huge, heartfelt thank you to the entire publishing team who helped bring *Garden Yourself Happy* to life. To Ru, Jessica, Molly and Caroline, your guidance, enthusiasm, encouragement and belief in this slightly chaotic, short-shorts-wearing gardener have meant the world. You made every step of the process feel supported and achievable, and I am genuinely grateful for the care you've shown this project.

To Claire and James, whose design and illustrations absolutely make this book – thank you. Your artwork brings the heart, humour and warmth of these pages to life in a way words alone never could. I think everyone reading this will see just how talented you are.

My thanks also go to the brilliant management team at Encanta. Charles, Rebecca, Grant, Amelia, Joe, Elizabeth and Georgina. You are the engine room behind so much of what I do. Thank you for your guidance, your strategy, your support and your ability to keep me grounded when life goes into overdrive. I'm lucky to have you all steering the ship with me.

And to my community, my followers, the people who've supported me from the first little garden video to the madness of all this, this book exists because of you. You're the ones who like, comment, share, laugh, message and show up again and again. You're the reason I get to do what I love every single day. You've encouraged me, challenged me, inspired me and kept me going when I've doubted myself.

Every video you've interacted with, every question you've asked, every moment you've shared, it all built this book. I cannot put into words how grateful I am for you. Thank you for believing in me, for backing me and for allowing me to share my garden, my life and my chaos with you. I hope this book gives you even a fraction of the joy you've given me.

From the bottom of my heart to everyone, thank you.

ABOUT THE AUTHOR

Jonny Hincks, best known online to his fans as @gardenwithjonny, is a Warwickshire-based gardening content creator, sharing his love for all things nature to his loyal following. Jonny's online content ranges from his best gardening tips, to showcasing his warm and silly sense of humour through fun reels outdoors. When Jonny isn't knee deep in soil, he works for the fire service, as a firefighter.

EBURY PRESS

UK | USA | Canada | Ireland | Australia
India | New Zealand | South Africa

Ebury Press is part of the Penguin Random House group of companies whose addresses can be found at global.penguinrandomhouse.com

Penguin Random House UK
One Embassy Gardens, 8 Viaduct Gardens, London SW11 7BW

penguin.co.uk

First published by Ebury Press in 2026

2

Copyright © Jonny Hincks 2026
Illustrations © James Yates
Author photo © Charlotte Wilson

The moral right of the author has been asserted.

Penguin Random House values and supports copyright. Copyright fuels creativity, encourages diverse voices, promotes freedom of expression and supports a vibrant culture. Thank you for purchasing an authorised edition of this book and for respecting intellectual property laws by not reproducing, scanning or distributing any part of it by any means without permission. You are supporting authors and enabling Penguin Random House to continue to publish books for everyone. No part of this book may be used or reproduced in any manner for the purpose of training artificial intelligence technologies or systems. In accordance with Article 4(3) of the DSM Directive 2019/790, Penguin Random House expressly reserves this work from the text and data mining exception.

Typeset by Claire Rochford

Printed and bound in Great Britain by Clays Ltd, Elcograf S.p.A.

The authorised representative in the EEA is Penguin Random House Ireland,
Morrison Chambers, 32 Nassau Street, Dublin D02 YH68

A CIP catalogue record for this book is available from the British Library

ISBN 9781529976243

 Penguin Random House is committed to a sustainable future for our business, our readers and our planet. This book is made from Forest Stewardship Council® certified paper.